FAITHFUL, CREATIVE, HOPEFUL

Fifteen Theses for Christians in a Crisis-Shaped World

JESSE A. ZINK

Church Publishing
19 East 34th Street
New York, NY 10016
www.churchpublishing.org

Cover design by Newgen
Typeset by Nord Compo

ISBN 978-1-64065-738-0 (paperback)
ISBN 978-1-64065-739-7 (eBook)

Library of Congress Control Number: 2024938955

To the Dio Community—

Faithful, Creative, Hopeful

CONTENTS

INTRODUCTION
Polycrisis and Christian Witness

This much seems clear: things are changing—rapidly.

When I was in elementary and middle school, the Berlin Wall was falling, the Cold War was ending, and the United States was emerging as the only global superpower. I grew into adulthood in what was, in retrospect, a charmed time: stable global politics, low inflation, increased global ties that facilitated a low cost of living, and a shared commitment to democratic norms and ideas. The threat of nuclear annihilation, which just a few years earlier had seemed pressing and existential, receded from public consciousness. Countries in the North Atlantic world reaped a "peace dividend" as they cooperated to reduce nuclear stockpiles. In the new millennium, as I emerged into adulthood, terrorist attacks shook western societies, and American, British, and Canadian soldiers fought wars in Iraq, Afghanistan, and elsewhere.[1] The damage and the response, however, came to feel divorced from the daily lives of many people, especially those who did not serve in the military. For many people, including me, it was possible to ignore the pressures and strains under which many people lived on a regular basis. The stability of this period generated enormous privilege for me and people like me—white, western, able-bodied, educated, and so on—indicated in our education, health, finances, and social welfare. While there were voices urging us to remember those who were being left behind or to care for the environment, that privilege allowed people like me to put aside these concerns for another day and not treat them with urgency.

Little of this is true any longer, even for those who enjoyed this sort of privileged stability in the past. There is a grueling land war in Europe. The United States is again locked in a rivalry with a nuclear power, though it is now China and not the Soviet Union, even as arms control agreements come to an end and nuclear weapons proliferate around the globe. Global ties continue to link the world together but rather than being seen as an unalloyed good, there are serious questions being raised about our interconnectedness. New nationalist movements are proclaiming the importance of ethnic identity, even as more people are on the move in the world than ever before. It is this movement, combined with dissatisfaction with global economic integration, that has led to a ferocious political reaction in some countries and in places a backsliding from democracy. Meanwhile, the economic model underlying the apparent prosperity of the years since the Cold War's end has had its imperfections revealed in a financial crash that cratered the global economy, significant income and wealth inequality, a growing housing crisis, and, now, proclamations of the fall of the American dream.[2] This inequality is present both within and between countries and is furthered by a set of market-based values that are spreading to new areas of life. Underlying all of this is an unignorable climate crisis in which flooding, wildfires, hurricanes, and heat waves are becoming an inescapable reality across the world, shaping lives and constraining opportunity. As if all this was not enough, the opening years of the third decade of the third millennium have been marked by a punishing global pandemic. We will not be able to pause and catch our breath. There is an urgency to this moment, and that urgency cannot be ignored.

This moment of urgency has brought prominence to a new word: polycrisis. First coined in the 1970s, the word has gained popularity among analysts and leaders looking at the challenges that global human society confronts. Polycrisis refers to the simultaneous occurrence of several crisis-level events—a list that includes pandemic, war, inflation, democratic decay, climate change, and more—that "interact so that the whole is even more overwhelming than the sum of the parts."[3] One of the lessons of studying history is that at many previous points in human existence, people have felt that their time was in some measure uniquely challenging and different from what had come before, that their era was a hinge period in human history. It is not surprising, therefore, that we might look at our moment and reach the same conclusion. Yet whether or not there is something unique about our moment is beside the point. History has given us this collection of crises. Our collective response will be shaped by many people in many places and across generations.

Thus, when I speak of "crisis-shaped" in this book, I am referring to the idea of polycrisis. My frame of reference for understanding these crises is primarily global—a crisis-shaped *world*. In this early part of the twenty-first century, humans are more connected to one another around the world than ever before. While different countries may have different local crises, my point of departure in this book is to understand this moment of polycrisis to be comprised of essentially three interlocking crises: climate, economics, and migration. Climate change—which I use as a shorthand to refer to a host of issues connected to a disordered relationship with creation, including pollution, environmental degradation, and biodiversity loss—is perhaps the greatest and most overriding consideration. The challenges it raises are, if not existential, of so great a magnitude that we are barely beginning to grasp them. Whole communities will be destroyed, patterns of life that we once depended on will be upended, and huge swathes of what we consider normal will be discarded. Indeed, all of this is happening now. Climate touches a whole host of other issues, and they are among the most basic to human existence. They include where we get the energy that powers our lives, how, what, and where we get the food that nourishes us, and how we relate to the natural world that surrounds us, even as we try to push it away.

When I think of climate, I increasingly tell myself that the climate situation is likely to continue to worsen for the rest of my life. I can only hope it will be improving by the time my children reach the end of theirs.

While there may once have been a time when market-based economics seemed a solution to many ills, that is no longer the case. The imperfections of the capitalist model in the form it has taken in recent decades—often called neoliberalism—are increasingly being revealed in inequality, the weakening of the public sphere, and perhaps most damagingly, the rise of a new set of denuded and debased values. Like climate, the dominance of this market-based model has implications in many other aspects of our lives, including how we govern ourselves, how we determine value, and how we relate to one another. Climate and economics are also related. The more we rely on a market-based model, the more we are driven to relate to our natural world in unsustainable and damaging ways. The more that climate change accelerates, the more that some people will take refuge in the self-protection mentality of the market.

Migration may seem the odd one out on this list, but its place is central. It is not a new phenomenon—far from it—but what is new is that already there are more people on the move than at most previous periods in history, and the number seems set only to grow. As climate change renders some parts of the world uninhabitable and neoliberal economics increases inequality between regions of the world, more and more people will continue to leave behind their homes to seek opportunity in other places, whether within their own country or in another. Again, migration has tremendous influences elsewhere. It can create significant human suffering and impose new burdens both on the places that people leave and the places where they seek a new home. More broadly, current waves of migration are changing the demographics of western societies and challenging human societies to grapple with new forms of difference and increased diversity.

We are no longer able to live in siloed ignorance of one another in the way previous generations could. People of different cultures and backgrounds will continue to come together in new ways. These encounters can be profoundly generative and creative. They can also be deeply damaging and destructive.

The ways in which these crises make themselves felt is different in different parts of the world. There are other crises as well, including mental health, systemic racism, poverty, gender-based violence and discrimination, housing, and so much else, and some of these will emerge in these pages.[4] My primary focus in this book, however, is on the braiding together of climate, economics, and migration, which I believe make this moment in global human history significant. They are at the core of the polycrisis to which we must respond.

* * *

In previous moments of uncertainty and instability in human history, people have turned to their religious faith for inspiration, guidance, and renewal. For many in the Euro-Atlantic world, this has meant turning to the Christian church. Yet what is clear about our moment is that it is not just human society that is changing, but the church too—and not for the better. In many ways, the institutional church in the North Atlantic world has never seemed weaker or less capable of rising to the moment. I grew up in an Episcopal church in the 1980s and 1990s. Though this was a largely secular community in New England, I was the beneficiary of a thriving Sunday school and a church that was packed full on Christmas and Easter. I was confirmed with about two dozen other young people, many of whom were part of an active youth group. When I look around the church in Montreal that I attend now, I am disoriented and confounded by the change. My children have never known a full church, not even on significant holidays, and have rarely known a Sunday school of sufficient size to justify more than a single, all-ages classroom. Churches that seemed to be full and thriving just a generation ago are today closing or merging with other congregations. Meanwhile, across the United States and Canada, as well as around the world, forms of Christianity have emerged that are closely tied to nationalism, masculine self-assertion, and social views misaligned with contemporary realities. There is a generalized sense that Christianity is either too old, tired, and enervated to respond to the moment, or that the answers it offers are so radically out-of-touch as to be harmful.

The COVID-19 pandemic that reached North America in 2020 was particularly damaging for the church because it restricted the church's ability to engage in its central task: gather people together in one place. The result of the pandemic has been an acceleration and deepening of some of these changes, forcing churches to adapt and modify their activities in ways they may never once have anticipated. The result among church members is varied, but often gives rise to further concern. Apathy, anxiety, disengagement, and drop-out are in evidence across the church. New statistical evidence is demonstrating the rapid drop-off in church membership and attendance in recent years. Average Sunday attendance across the Episcopal Church has dropped more than forty percent from 2013 to 2022. In 2019, a report in the Anglican Church of Canada predicted that on current trends there would not be any Anglicans left in Canada by 2040. It seems likely that the pandemic has only accelerated this trend. A preliminary report in Canada, for instance, documented decreases in attendance in some dioceses of twenty-five to fifty percent between 2019 and 2022.[5] Similar declines are evident in other denominations as well. Jesus himself told his followers that the gates of hell would not prevail against his church (Matt. 16:18). But sometimes church institutions can look pretty precarious.

I am a child of this church. I was baptized as an infant in the Anglican Church of Canada and raised from a young age in an

Episcopal church in the United States. I have lived, travelled, and worked with Christians in many parts of the world and presently live and work in Montreal as principal of an ecumenical theological college. This belonging to the church has nurtured and continues to form me in the ways of the Christian faith and left in me an abiding love for the gospel of Jesus Christ as expressed in the Anglican tradition. Through the Anglican tradition, variously expressed, I find my relationship with God in Jesus Christ sustained and deepened and I am called into loving engagement and service in the world in which I find myself. My upbringing and the faith it gave me also left me with a deep affection for the churches of this Anglican tradition. When I join in the creeds of the church in affirming that I believe in "one, holy, catholic, and apostolic church," I often find myself placing the emphasis on "believe." I believe in the existence of such a church because I have seen it and encountered it in the world. I place my trust in this church—even in spite of its association with retrograde social causes or seeming status as an irrelevancy—because I have found in it a way of living that leads to fullness and wholeness of life. I believe the church still has gifts to offer to a world in need of them.

This is the context in which I offer this book. It is born both from concern about the seemingly intractable global crises of our time and concern about where the church finds itself in response. But it is also born from the great sense of possibility and expectation about what Christians can offer to a hurting and changing world. Rather than being enervated or out-of-touch, I find that what the Christian faith can offer the world is ideas, practices, and ways of being that point the path toward a fullness of life that to many people no longer seems possible.

* * *

I have structured this book as a series of theses: declarative statements that arise from my understanding of this moment of polycrisis, the Christian faith, and my experience of the life of the church in these last years. Each chapter begins with a thesis which I then illustrate and substantiate. Those familiar with Christian history will know the occasionally august place of the thesis. Most famously, the German monk Martin Luther reputedly nailed ninety-five theses to the door of a church in Wittenberg in 1517. (While he definitely wrote the theses, it is unclear if he actually put them on the door.) Theses of this nature were a common method at the time to invite debate. Luther succeeded, probably more than he ever imagined. His ninety-five theses were an early touchstone for the Protestant Reformation. I do not claim any such grand intentions. I have chosen the thesis as a structural tool because its declarative nature provides, as Luther knew, something to engage with and react to. I have also chosen it because it provides a framework by which to touch on a wide variety of topics and their interconnections, even as I know that some of these theses could be an entire book on their own. Despite the range of topics, however, these theses are not meant say everything that needs to be said about Christian witness. Perhaps ironically given my work, I have very little to say here about the ministry of the church, for instance, though this occupies much of my professional life. As it was for Luther, then, this collection of theses is not the last word on a subject. In this book, I have deliberately sought to introduce a range of topics as a contribution to a discussion and an invitation for response.

My goal in offering these theses is not to provide practical guidance on precisely what shape the Christian church and Christian ministry should take in coming years. Each Christian community exists in a unique context that will shape its future. Rather, what I am doing is drawing on Christian history, theology, Scripture, and ministry to offer ideas and challenges that I hope readers will be able to adapt for their own contexts as they respond to our challenging global situation. Change in the church will come, I believe, not from implementing a new, transformative set of practices—I don't think any single set of such practices exist—but from new thinking, new acting, and new being grounded in a shared tradition. It is that thinking, acting, and being which I hope this book spurs.

Overarching all of these theses are the words I have used as the book's title: *faithful, creative, hopeful.* Each has an important meaning and offers an interpretive key to each thesis, even if I do not always explicitly reference them. By faithful, I mean a kind of groundedness in our Christian tradition. Faithful means that we need to be able to draw from the wealth of resources provided by our Christian forebears in the two millennia since Christ's birth. It also means that we need to be grounded in Christian practices of prayer, service, and worship. By creative, I mean that Christians need to be experimental and open to the new possibilities that the Holy Spirit is constantly unfolding in our midst. The COVID-19 pandemic has taught us much about the meaning of risk. The church, I hope, in its nature as a supportive and encouraging community, can always be a safe place to take risk and try new things. By hopeful, I mean that Christians are called to constantly be looking to what God is doing now and looking forward to what God will do in the future. This is not a facile optimism that suggests everything will work out just fine. But neither is it a resigned cynicism that counsels resignation and despair. Hope is instead a defiant ethic that holds on when all else seems lost, confident that God is acting in our midst. Hope allows us to risk now, act now, knowing that defeat is not the last word for God.

To the frustration of readers ever since, Martin Luther's ninety-five theses were one continuous list, with no divisions or sections to help the reader make sense of the overall argument. Though I only have fifteen theses, I have grouped them into four sections: apocalyptic clarity, resistant ethos, resistant practice, and renewed church. The meaning of these sections will become clear as each unfolds. In brief, however, the first set of theses—apocalyptic clarity—offers a uniquely, though oft-ignored, scriptural approach to seeing the world that is attentive to powers that work against Christian witness. The second and third—resistant ethos and resistant practice—offer ideas and practices that can orient Christian communities to live in a resistant fashion to these powers. The final section—renewed church—pays specific attention to the church to consider pathways to new life. To be sure, some of these divisions can be artificial—the line between ethos and practice, for instance, is not always clear—but I hope these divisions will help the reader through these theses.

Two final words are in order. First, while my experience of the Christian church is broader and more diverse than it is for many, when I speak about the church in this book I have primarily in mind what is often called the mainline or historic denominations of North America, of which the Episcopal Church and Anglican Church of Canada to which I belong are examples. I lived out the years of the pandemic as part of the Anglican Church of Canada in the specific context of the city of Montreal and the province of Quebec. Christians in Quebec have often taken a perverse pride in the extreme and aggressive secularism of our context, a result of a religious history in this province that is unique in North America. Religious trends have a habit of unfolding first here before spreading to the rest of the continent. At the same time, my ministry as a theological educator has naturally kept me in touch with many different parts of the church in Canada and beyond. It is from this context—rooted in Quebec's particularity and in conversation with other parts of the church—that I offer this book.

Finally, as should be clear, I write in this book from a position of deep concern and care for the church. As such, I often write about the Christian community in these pages. However, my deeper concern is about the nature of Christian witness that undergirds expressions of the church. This Christian witness is founded in the good news—gospel—of Jesus Christ, the deposit of faith that has been handed down across the centuries, through the church, to those of us in this generation who have the privilege of proclaiming it anew. Part of the proof of the truth of this gospel, I believe, is that it has been kept alive across these centuries by a church that is fallible, imperfect, and always under strain. It is this gospel that will always be relevant to the human condition, and it is this gospel that Christians are called to live and proclaim in crisis-shaped times. Our primary focus as Christians must be not the survival of our existing church institutions, as comforting as we find them. Instead, the church now and once again in crisis itself can truly live in solidarity with a crisis-shaped world by sharing a gospel message that remains both deeply and profoundly good and excitingly and disturbingly new, as much now as it was when it was first incarnated and preached in Galilee two thousand years ago.

"The gates of hell will not prevail against it," Jesus said of his church. Indeed. At a time when the gates of hell can seem frighteningly close and the church somewhat wobbly in its response, may Christ's words inspire and comfort us, and may these theses offer some contribution to the Christian witness in a world in polycrisis.

APOCALYPTIC CLARITY

THESIS ONE

A crisis-shaped world requires apocalyptic clarity

Martin Luther King, Jr. delivered the last Sunday morning sermon of his life from the pulpit of Washington National Cathedral. In it, he invoked a phrase he had used throughout his ministry: "the arc of the moral universe is long, but it bends toward justice."[1] Two generations later, Barack Obama often used the same words to describe his work as president of the United States. It is easy to see why both men drew on these words. They articulate the unfinishedness of their moments: society is not yet wholly just. But they also do not necessarily propose radical action. It is bending, not necessarily breaking, with the past. To get where society needs to go, the words implicitly indicate, we just need to keep altering things a little bit here and there. The saying is also impersonal: it bends. Who is doing the bending? It's not clear.

To differing degrees, part of the success of King and Obama was their appeals to white, well-educated, social-justice-oriented liberals who liked to think of themselves as being on the right side of history. The arc of the moral universe is long but it bends toward . . . the end of legal segregation and voting rights for all. The arc of the moral universe is long but it bends toward . . . same-sex marriage and expanded access to health insurance. Indeed, Obama's election itself seemed a confirmation of these very words. A country so deeply deformed by racism had elected a black man to its highest office. I am a white, well-educated, comfortably living more-or-less liberal who likes to think of myself as being on the right side of history and who cheered Obama's inauguration. It's not surprising that these words resonated with me during his presidency. "Yes," I thought, "he's right. We can see it bending before our eyes." Part of the appeal was the impersonality. One could almost conclude that the arc of the moral universe will just take care of itself on its path toward justice. This led to a further implication, left unacknowledged but lurking not far away: "And I don't need to change much for it to happen."

It is hard to have this serene confidence in a crisis-shaped world. The arc of the moral universe is long and is bending toward dramatic climate change. It is bending toward the destruction of whole communities by wildfire—from Fort McMurray in Alberta to Paradise in California to Lahaina in Hawaii and many others around the world. New words and phrases, like "heat dome," "atmospheric river," or "firestorm," are entering our lexicon and demonstrating how events that were once rare are now occurring with frightening regularity. This nonstop "crazy" weather is a clear indication of the damage done to the planet by human-caused climate change. Our collective resistance to change our ways and restructure where we source our energy is a testament to the power of fossil fuel consumption and commitment to convenience that is proving frighteningly hard to break.

The arc of the moral universe may be long, but it is bending toward ever greater inequality and violence. More than a decade ago, I marched in protest after Trayvon Martin was shot by George Zimmerman in Florida, one of only many young black men who have been unjustly killed either by private citizens or police officers. In Montreal, I marched in protest after the Indigenous woman Joyce Echaquan died in hospital, just a few days after livestreaming on social media the mockery, hostility, and dismissiveness she encountered from health care workers. Echaquan was only one of many Indigenous people—and especially Indigenous women—in Canada who have suffered from the racism and inequality that is part of the structure of Canadian society. These lists of names are far too long: not just Trayvon Martin but Michael Brown, Breonna Taylor, George Floyd, and more; not just Joyce Echaquan but Pamela George, Colton Booshie, Barbara Kentner, or any of the scores of little known missing and murdered Indigenous women in Canada. For a population that had previously been able to ignore the horrors of the residential school system in Canada, the uncovering of hundreds of unmarked graves at the sites of former residential schools beginning in 2021 was a stark unveiling of the reality of the injustice with which Indigenous people have been treated in Canada. Each of these deaths testifies to the embedded power of racism and a society that systematically privileges the interests and needs of white people over those of others.

Our global world is shrinking as people in formerly distant parts of the world have begun to seek new homes in other countries which have decidedly mixed opinions about this movement. This has caused political anxiety and turmoil in our societies and hardship and death for many on the move. The arc of the moral universe is long but it is bending toward capsized boats in the Mediterranean, migrants in indefinite limbo in camps in Greece, Turkey, or Libya, and the body of a little boy washed up on a beach. Meanwhile, the arc of the moral universe may be long, but it is bending toward ever greater control by a smaller number of individuals and corporations. We increasingly rely on a small handful of technology companies for our daily existence. In exchange, they store away ever more of our personal data with little oversight or thought about how it may one day be used. The arc of the moral universe is long but it is bending toward a world with new centers of concentrated power that are increasingly opaque and unaccountable. Both widespread migration and the rise of major multinational corporations are testimonies to the power of an economic model that concentrates wealth, exacerbates inequality, and creates tremendous incentives for people to undertake dangerous movement to seek new opportunities.

Obama and King were clear-eyed about the obstacles to social progress in their time and worked hard to overcome these. By contrast, the gradualism and impersonality implied by many uses of "the arc of the moral universe is long" can sometimes seem a bit naïve and out-of-touch with the reality of a crisis-shaped world. To change this, we need to pay attention to what works against the abundance and wholeness of life that God offers to God's people. That means that Christians need to pay attention to power.

* * *

Shortly after pointing to the arc of the moral universe on that Sunday morning at the National Cathedral, Martin Luther King concluded his sermon by quoting the last book of the Bible: "Thank God for John," he said, "who centuries ago out on a lonely, obscure island called Patmos caught vision of a new Jerusalem descending out of heaven from God, who heard a voice saying, 'Behold, I make all things new—former things are passed away.'" King was quoting Revelation, the record of the visions of a Christian man named John who lived at a time of great persecution a couple of generations after Jesus. Revelation is part of a broader tradition of Christian writing, building on Jewish tradition, that is intensely attuned to power, particularly the powers in the world that obstruct God's reign. It is called apocalyptic writing, from a Greek word that means "unveiling" or "revelation." The operative word in apocalyptic writing, and one often used in Revelation, is see. An apocalyptic text allows those who can see properly to understand what is happening in the world. It reveals the activity of powers and gives meaning to events that seem challenging or out-of-control.

While Revelation is the classic Christian apocalyptic work, it is also likely the book that has caused more interpretive angst than any other in the Bible. Throughout the history of the church, some Christians have thrilled to it and found in it decisive shape to their faith. Other Christians have approached it more warily, if they approached it at all. Revelation may be trying to offer an unveiling and demonstration of what is really happening in the world of its readers, but it is easy for the modern reader to be suspicious of its incredible visions of angels, beasts, heavenly hosts, four horsemen, seven seals, and a new Jerusalem descending to earth. It can all seem just a bit too far-fetched to be of much value. For a time, this is how I found myself approaching Revelation. If the answers it gave in its unveiling were so unfamiliar and confounding, it seemed to have little to offer to Christians today.

Apocalyptic works have an audience in mind. Revelation was not written for the comfortable and well-off. It was not written for social justice types whose hearts stir when they hear "The arc of the moral universe is long but it bends toward justice." In a word, it was not written for people like me, the economically and socially privileged. Apocalyptic literature has often been described as "a literature of the oppressed."[2] It is written for those who find themselves marginalized in society, with little hope for change through human means. It is precisely because of this marginalization that the first readers of works like Revelation would find explanations of what was really happening and visions of God's future action to be so meaningful.

John likely wrote Revelation at a time when followers of Jesus were feeling the oppression of the Roman Empire through persecution, arrest, and abuse. Indeed, the infamous mark of the beast in Revelation—the number 666—may be a coded reference to Nero, the megalomaniacal Roman emperor. In Revelation, Babylon, an ancient kingdom that had once taken the Jewish people into exile, now serves as a metaphor for Rome. Babylon is depicted as a beast who rules cruelly over the earth, killing, imprisoning, blaspheming. At a time when the Roman Empire trumpeted the *Pax Romana*, the stability it brought to the world, Revelation's depiction confronts Rome head-on. It is not peaceful; it is murderous. It is not stable; it is chaotic. It is not prosperous; it only succeeds by force.

Revelation's conclusion is clear. After a lengthy battle, an angel proclaims: "Fallen, fallen is Babylon the great!" (Rev. 18:2). In other words, the Roman Empire and the persecution it embodies will not endure. Revelation then concludes with a beautiful vision: "Then I saw a new heaven and a new earth. . . . And I saw a holy city, the new Jerusalem, coming down out of heaven from God." John hears a voice saying, "See the home of God is among mortals. He will dwell with them. . . . he will wipe every tear from their eyes. Death will be no more; mourning and crying and pain will be no more." Then John hears the words that King and so many others have found inspiration in: "See, I am making all things new." (Rev. 21:1–5). It is a majestic vision of a world transformed, of the ruler of the universe coming to dwell on earth, of a new heavenly city descending to replace all that has come before. Not only does God demonstrate God's sovereignty and power by defeating Babylon but God replaces Babylon with a new Jerusalem and establishes God's reign of righteousness forevermore. Here, there is nothing about a moral arc that impersonally bends in any which direction. Instead, what is revealed is that God is the decisive actor who conclusively defeats what stands in the way of abundant life. It is God who is bending the arc of the universe, not toward mere justice but toward the final perfection of all things. To a people who were suffering, uncertain, and fearful about what the future might bring, the unveiling of the truth that John offered would have been hopeful and transforming. God would defeat Rome. The Lamb on the throne would conquer. God would dwell in the new Jerusalem in their midst. This apocalyptic vision revealed hope, possibility, and new creation.

Revelation is the most explicitly and thorough-going apocalyptic book of the New Testament but it is far from the only place where the apocalyptic vision appears. It was characteristic of much of the early church. The letter to the Ephesians, for instance, understands Christian living to take place within a sphere affected by heavenly contestation between good and evil. At the start of the letter, the reader is reminded of the great power of God, demonstrated above all in Christ's resurrection: "God put this power to work in Christ when he raised him from the dead and seated him at his right hand in the heavenly places, far above all rule and authority and power and dominion, and above every name that is named, not only in this age but also in the age to come" (Eph. 1:20–21). This power supports Christians in their struggle against the forces in the world that work against God, as we are reminded at the letter's end: "For our struggle is not against enemies of blood and flesh, but against the rulers, against the authorities, against the cosmic powers of this present darkness, against the spiritual forces of evil in the heavenly places" (Eph. 6:12).

The words "rulers" and "authorities" are elsewhere translated as "principalities and powers" and have come to summarize the opposition the Christian message encounters in the world. In between these opening and closing chapters of Ephesians, we are given an extended description of the fullness of life to which God calls his followers, a life marked by the breaking down of barriers, by interdependence and mutuality, and by growing together into the full maturity toward which God is calling us. But Ephesians reminds us that this Christian witness is not stymied simply by recalcitrant or uninterested individuals but by great forces, which can be not just temporal but cosmic and spiritual as well. Apocalyptic literature reveals not only that God is acting and acting in ways that bring hope and new life but that there are forces of opposition that are actively working against Christian witness. It is these powers and principalities that must be defeated for God's people to realize fullness of life.

* * *

But so what? John's visions in Revelation did not lead to the overthrow of the Roman Empire. Rome continued to expand its reach around the world and Christians continued to be persecuted. Talking about the powers and principalities can seem like a bunch of pious guff if it doesn't actually lead to overturning those powers. Indeed, it could be harmful. If apocalyptic literature encourages us to view our opponents as demonic or representing a dark power, it may obstruct the kind of incremental progress that often leads to change. Moreover, there is still the challenge of Revelation and its vision of an apocalypse that can seem far-fetched. And it's not just the destruction. Talking about a new heaven and a new earth can seem pretty far away from the brokenness of the world as many people experience it.

The great gift of apocalyptic literature is the imaginative vision it offers. Revelation's persuasiveness was rooted in how it saw the world. John saw clearly the violence and empty promises of the Roman Empire. He saw clearly that the world is deeply marked and marred by human sinfulness and brokenness. He saw clearly that human action on its own was insufficient to address the real problems that Christians encountered. It is possible to see apocalyptically—to be attuned to and aware of the powers of this world—without endorsing every last vision of the apocalypse contained in Scripture. Indeed, this apocalyptic seeing is vital. If we cannot see clearly that powers and principalities continue to exist in our midst today—however hidden and opaque they may be—then it does not matter which direction the moral universe is heading because it simply will not bend. To live apocalyptically is first of all to have the clarity to see that the powers in the world who promise strength, stability, and prosperity are purveyors of false goods. Instead of abundant life, they offer death.

Apocalyptic thinking does not stop there. After recognizing the truth of the powers of this world and the reality of God's continued action, we are then led to a new place: hope. In some ways this sounds perverse: seeing the world in terms of overmighty and unaccountable powers could lead some people toward despair. But Christian hope is not a warm and fuzzy feeling about the bending of a moral arc toward justice. Christian hope, as I will develop further in a later thesis, is a countervailing power to the powers of this world that sees the world clearly for what it is—beset by inequality and injustice, or in a word, beset by crises. Seeing this clearly, hope leads Christians to live now as it will one day be: in mutuality, in peace, in forgiveness. For Christians, hope is based not in the thought that they will be whisked away to some other-worldly heaven. Hope comes from the promise that in God's final fulfillment God's city comes down to earth and renews our world. In that city, there is a tree of life with an abundance of fruit and leaves that are meant "for the healing of the nations" (Rev. 22:2). There is a spring and it contains the "water of life" (Rev. 21:6). It is a city in which God dwells with healing and restoration.

But there is at least one last problem. Well-educated, social justice types have never been the intended audience of apocalyptic literature. The appeal of a gradualist politics to people like me may be that it never truly threatens the privilege and wealth I enjoy. If I benefit from the powers and principalities of this world—as I assuredly do—and if everything seems rather stable and peaceful, then I may have little interest in developing the apocalyptic imagination. My privilege means I am a late arrival to apocalyptic clarity. Indigenous people in North America, for instance, have for some time pointed out that they already live in an apocalyptic reality and have been doing so for the five centuries since Europeans first arrived.[3]

But this may be the great gift of a crisis-shaped world to a complacent church. In an age of a climate crisis and a migration crisis, of anonymous algorithms and globe-spanning corporations, and so many other manifestations of the powers and principalities, Christians cannot sleepwalk through the world and wait for a return to "normal." This would leave us oblivious to our painful realities and systemic oppressions and ignorant of the powers and principalities. Instead, Christian witness begins by reclaiming an apocalyptic clarity. This means recognizing the nature of the world in which we live, understanding the depth of its deformation, and remaining convinced of God's action for justice and judgment. It is clarity and imagination that allow us to see clearly our crisis-shaped world and so work for the day when we hear those transformative words ringing clearly across the land: "Behold, I am making all things new."

THESIS TWO

Economic structures are the greatest obstacle to Christian witness

For her book, *On the Clock: What Low-Wage Work Did to Me and How It Drives America Insane*, the journalist Emily Guendelsberger spent time working at three low-wage jobs across America: an Amazon warehouse in Indiana, a call center in North Carolina, and a McDonald's in San Francisco. For the last of these jobs, she found a room in an apartment of a friend of a friend of a friend in Oakland. The room had fleas and was directly over a church gymnasium, but it made for a straightforward commute to her job. It also turned out that her new roommate was the choir director in the church. Guendelsberger had played piano in her church choir as a teenager and was elated. She didn't know anyone in the Bay Area and joining the choir seemed like a great way to meet new people and nurture one of her passions.

It didn't work out. Soon after starting at McDonald's, she realized she would have to quit the choir. Her work schedule would often be posted less than a day before the week began and she could never predict how many or which hours she would be scheduled for. Committing to a regular weekday evening rehearsal time, not to mention a Sunday morning church service, was impossible. Even if her work schedule had a little more predictability, her shifts left her completely exhausted. She was constantly on her feet at McDonald's and the breaks were barely sufficient to catch her breath. Her commute was long and when she got home all she wanted to do was sleep. She wanted to be part of a church community. Her work simply wouldn't let her. She writes, "It would be tough to have hobbies under these conditions, and nearly *impossible* to hold down a second job. Yet again, I can't imagine how people with kids make this work."[1]

Guendelsberger's book, like Barbara Ehrenreich's *Nickel and Dimed* a generation ago, is an important piece of reporting on the reality of low-wage work. What it makes clear is that for many workers in the modern economy, one's life centers on one's work—but that the job is an inconstant and unfaithful friend. Work schedules are unpredictable, varying in number of hours per week or days or shifts worked, all apparently dependent on capricious algorithms that allot shifts according to little discernible logic. The rates of pay are so low relative to the cost of living that workers need to spend virtually all their time thinking either about work or about survival—how to pay for unexpected medical expenses, how to keep a roof over one's head, how to keep a car going. There is no time left over for hobbies, passions, community, or, well, church. As Guendelsberger's subtitle makes clear, the stress of this economic model has tremendous impacts on workers. Even after just a few weeks of working in a call center and trying to sell new services to people who were calling for help she was unable to provide, she found herself breaking down and unable to cope mentally. When she worked at McDonald's, her breaks were timed to the second, leaving her with inadequate time to eat or refresh herself before she had to return to work. There was a timekeeping device that kept track of how long it took to fill each order, meaning she and her fellow staff were constantly under pressure. She reports that McDonald's had determined just how many staff were necessary to provide a minimum level of service during rush periods, and then provided only that amount of staff, further compounding the pressure. It is no wonder that she was exhausted at the end of her shift. Everything about the work environment was oriented toward enriching the company for which she worked, with little attention to the cost that the system imposed on her.

While the low-wage workers that Guendelsberger introduces the reader to and whose ranks she joins for a time bear the brunt of this economic logic in particularly acute fashion, it is a logic that affects many people. Families with one or more college-educated workers may once have been able to survive on one full-time income, leaving one member of the family—generally the wife—to attend to the myriad of responsibilities associated with raising children, having a social life, participating in community, and, yes, belonging to church. No family model was ever perfect, and this model was often most true of white families. But in large measure, community (and church) life in North America in the period after the Second World War developed around the expectation that some member of the family—again, usually the wife—would have disposable time and disposable income to help keep voluntary organizations, like altar guilds, choirs, and Sunday schools, going. Twenty years ago, however, Senator Elizabeth Warren and her coauthor and daughter, Amelia Tyagi, were already calling out the "two-income trap," in which families felt they needed both spouses to be working to generate enough income to sustain the family's life, but that the extra income did not cover the added expenses that came with losing the flexibility offered by a nonworking spouse.[2]

For some people, especially well-educated professionals in secure employment, the years of the COVID-19 pandemic have been an opportunity to reassess their lives and think about how much work they really want to be doing. The unionization movements and strikes that have taken place in the pandemic's aftermath—across both traditional blue-collar jobs like car manufacturing as well as white-collar workers in media, education, entertainment, and other fields and new sites like Starbucks cafes or Amazon warehouses—are another indication that many workers are realizing that the current system is not working for them, though none of these labor actions have yet significantly changed the flexible working conditions and difficult jobs that Guendelsberger documents. Except for a privileged few, fundamental change in the economy seems a long way off—and it's a long way off precisely because of the immense power of a certain set of economic structures. If we are to address this, we must recognize the nature of this power and the obstacle it poses to Christian witness.

* * *

I have already suggested that one of the primary features of a crisis-shaped world is our economic structures. On one level, this may seem strange. Wage labor and market economies are not new inventions. In one way or another, humans have been structuring their economic lives together for most of recorded human history. But what has changed, and changed rather significantly in the past two generations, is the reach of these market structures, their depth and intensity, and the power accorded them. The combined effect has been to give new salience to market-based considerations in more domains of our common life, marginalize other aspects of our shared existence—like religion—and promote a set of values that are antithetical to a Christian worldview.

Broadly speaking, in the decades after the Second World War, there was a consensus in many western countries that the government should play some role in the economy and the shaping of our common life. In Canada, England, and other countries, this led to the development of publicly funded universal health care, large investments in public education, strong unions, publicly owned companies, public pensions, and government regulation of private industry. On an international level, western countries created multilateral institutions like the World Bank and the International Monetary Fund to help stabilize countries in distress and expand the reach of this model. Much of this activity was underlain by the beliefs of the economist John Maynard Keynes and went under the heading of Keynesianism. Government was a public good, it was believed, and it had a central role to play in shaping aspects of shared life in western societies.[3]

Beginning in the 1960s and then gathering momentum during the economic difficulties of the 1970s, this economic model came under pressure from a different economic vision. The politicians who carried these views forward were new leaders like Ronald Reagan, president of the United States from 1981 to 1989; Margaret Thatcher, prime minister of England from 1979 to 1990; and Brian Mulroney, prime minister of Canada from 1984 to 1992. To varying extents, each of these leaders and the people they appointed viewed their job as removing government's role from as many aspects of society as possible and allowing a freer rein to economic decision-making. As Reagan famously (or infamously) said, the nine most terrifying words in the English language are, "I'm from the government and I'm here to help."[4] In a similar vein, Thatcher deplored the number of people seeking help from the government and society: "And who is society? There is no such thing! There are individual men and women and there are families."[5] The basic unit that the government should care about was primarily individual and small-scale. These individuals and families could be trusted to make the decisions that were best for them. Together, these leaders believed, these decisions would produce a well-functioning and prosperous society. Reagan, Thatcher, and Mulroney pursued policy agendas that included deregulating many industries that had previously been subject to government regulation and privatizing state-owned industries and letting them survive (or not) as private companies. They weakened unions and lowered tax rates in ways that particularly benefited the wealthy. They also pursued free trade agreements, seeking to expand the global reach of trade and so lower prices for consumers. In the 1990s, ostensibly left-leaning politicians like Tony Blair, Jean Chrétien, and Bill Clinton generally tended to confirm—and not challenge—these policy achievements. It was Bill Clinton who proclaimed, in an echo of Reagan, that "the era of big government is over."[6] It was Tony Blair who took the radical step of introducing fees for university students, thus undoing a long-standing view that higher education was a public good from which all society benefited, not just those who happened to be students.

The triumph of this economic model coincided with the end of the Cold War. Not only had western democracies triumphed over the authoritarian Soviets. Western capitalism, it was believed, had decisively triumphed over communism. The political scientist Francis Fukuyama called it "the end of history."[7] What he meant was that people had discovered the "final form of human government": a market-based liberal democracy in which the state played a minimal role and maximized freedom and choice for individuals. The only task now was to extend this model around the world so everyone could share in its benefits. The help that the World Bank and the IMF offered to developing countries now came with the expectation and requirement that these countries adopt similar policies: privatize state industries, shrink the size of the state, lower tax rates, and generally reduce the role of government, a set of policies that became known as the "Washington Consensus." Along with the expansion of the World Trade Organization (WTO) and the reduction of global barriers to trade, it came to dominate the policy agenda of many countries. Through free trade and lax antitrust enforcement, corporations began to grow to previously unimaginable size, straddling the world and delivering services to huge parts of the human population.

During the 1990s and the first part of the twenty-first century, the word most often used to describe this economic consensus was globalization, a world I will return to in a subsequent thesis. Now the word more commonly used is neoliberalism. Each, in their own way, is accurate. Neoliberalism is a broad term that indicates how these economic ideas are related to earlier eighteenth- and nineteenth-century ideas about freedom and individuals. The neo- in the word is an indication of the way the ideas' proponents thought they were reclaiming and updating these older ideas. But it is clear now that neoliberalism took older ideas and turbocharged them beyond recognition. Economic ideas moved beyond the realm of business and into areas that were previously seen to be beyond their reach. Take, for instance, the very human act of standing in line. Standing in line may not always be the most comfortable experience, but it has often been deemed to be a fair way of allocating scarce goods. A neoliberal mindset rooted in a belief in the power of markets, by contrast, asks if people who have the means should be able to pay money to buy their way out of having to stand in line. The answer, as anyone who has traveled through an airport filled with Nexus and Pre-Check lanes can attest, is now clear: of course! A market for access to security lines has been created and those who are willing and able to pay for speedier access should be able to do so. It is not just security lines, of course. Major corporations now create markets for access to concert tickets, airplane seats, and any number of other goods for which standing in line was once the option. It is not surprising: the dominant policy response has for a generation or more been this: when in doubt, create a market and let individuals and corporations sort it out for themselves. The political philosopher Michael Sandel calls our era a period of market triumphalism. We have moved from *having* a market-based economy to *being* a market-based society. The difference, he argues, is that "a market economy is a tool—a valuable and effective tool—for organizing productive activity. A market society is a way of life in which market values seep into every aspect of human endeavor. It's a place where social relations are made over in the image of the market."[8]

On the surface, neoliberalism and its attendant market society can appear to produce many benefits. If I think of myself as a consumer—and this is precisely how neoliberalism wants me to think of myself—then the benefits are obvious. More and more products from more and more places around the world are available to me at lower and lower prices. A globalized economic order has also spread wealth around the world. As China and other Asian countries have become factories to the world, the extent of extreme poverty has been reduced. The trouble with this logic is that no one is only a consumer. We are also people who need, for instance, jobs. The harsh nature of the current labor system is a steep price to pay for those low prices. Moreover, it is becoming clear that many of the costs of a neoliberal economic order have been masked. A world of globalization depends on cheap energy to move people and things around the world. But if that cheap energy is fueled by fossil fuels that are warming the atmosphere, then the costs of this system may not be so low after all. It may be that we just have not yet paid the full price—in the form of out-of-control weather, storm damage, and more.

Neoliberalism has had a four-decade run in western societies but the consensus around it may be fraying. During the pandemic governments took extraordinary steps to intervene in the economy. The administrations of both Donald Trump and Joe Biden in the United States have advanced policy agendas that have questioned key neoliberal tenets, and these questions are being echoed in other countries. But the impacts of neoliberalism remain. Corporations wield outsize power. Welfare states have frayed. Income and wealth inequality have risen, as a small number of privileged people capture the gains of a system that impoverishes many others. Even if the neoliberal consensus is coming to an end, the market-based society it bequeathed us remains firmly intact. Guendelsberger's story, with which I began, shows just how entrenched the system is. McDonald's, perhaps the quintessential global corporation, has developed a system in which it can predict the minimal amount of staffing it needs and then schedule staff at seemingly haphazard times to meet those needs. There is little regard for the needs of the employee or any sense of loyalty to that person. No wonder job turnover is so high. No wonder the work system is imposing significant strain on people. It is a system that is designed to produce economic wealth for corporations and their owners by minimizing their costs and maximizing their revenue. It is a logic that has been taken too far, too often.

* * *

It is one thing to describe an economic model and its power in the world. It is another to suggest, as I have in this thesis, that it is an obstacle to Christian witness. To understand this claim, however, it is helpful to think in terms of what I have already suggested about apocalyptic clarity and powers and principalities. In short, neoliberalism and the market-based society it creates is a power and principality in this world that is working against God's action for wholeness of life. To be clear, I make this claim specifically about current economic models and their broad societal influence, not about market-based economies as a general tool for structuring aspects of human interaction. I will develop this in several subsequent theses but in the rest of this chapter, I focus on two related claims to begin to demonstrate how economic structures serve as obstacles. First, neoliberalism propounds a set of values that are antithetical to Christian witness. Second, neoliberalism is increasingly taking on the functions of religion in society and in so doing further marginalizing Christian witness.

Part of the seductive nature of neoliberalism is that it often seems to be free of values. The implicit—and sometimes explicit—invitation is to enter a world where people do not need to worry about clashing beliefs or values. Instead, we can simply worry about a single thing: price. When in doubt, the neoliberal answer is clear: establish a market and the price that is established between a buyer and seller is the only value that matters. It used to be that some sports stadiums took on names that reflected the values of a community or the people who were important in that community. As a child, I was transfixed by the opening of the SkyDome, the baseball field in Toronto with a retractable roof. Part of my obsession was with the name, which evoked the wonders of that engineering achievement (even if the roof didn't always work quite right). There was also Three Rivers Stadium where the Pittsburgh Pirates played baseball. It was a name that spoke directly to the location of the stadium and the historic importance of that community's relationship with the natural world around it. Names like these rarely exist anymore. Instead, naming rights are sold to the highest bidder. This is virtually always a corporation that wants to draw attention to itself. Instead of the SkyDome, it is now the Rogers Centre. Instead of Three Rivers Stadium, it is now PNC Park, named after the company which is the Pirates' official "naming rights partner." A market was created—the stadium offered to sell its name—and buyers appeared. The only value that matters is the price that is created. What doesn't matter is anything reflecting the history, location, or broader community in which the stadium is located, or inspiring awe in young children. By relying only on price, a market-based society both sidesteps and marginalizes questions about value that might be more difficult to resolve but in which communities have historically found meaning.

From a Christian perspective, these all amount to troubling claims. Like many other religious traditions—and indeed like many secular traditions—Christians claim that there are values beyond that of price. The creation story tells us that human beings have an innate dignity that comes from being made in the image of God. The vision of Christian community developed in the writings of the New Testament prizes interdependence and mutual giving and receiving, not individual freedom. Jesus' teachings call for people to care for those who are left behind or left out. This may be one of the clearest contradictions of all between Christianity and a market-based society: Jesus made clear that at the core of his ministry was the proclamation of good news to the poor. Not always successfully, the church has sought to keep this before it ever since. In a market-based society by contrast, increasingly the only value that matters is price. I may want to cut to the front of the airport security line but if I cannot afford to pay for Nexus or Pre-Check, well, tough luck. The reach of a market-based society means the implications are about a lot more than waiting in line. When housing policy moves from the question of putting a roof over everyone's head to promoting housing as an investable asset that serves as a reliable route to income and wealth and is subject solely to supply and demand, then who gets housing depends solely on who is able to pay. In a market-based society to be poor is to be disadvantaged and left out. When markets extend into ever further realms of our life then the consequences of this poverty are significant and cascading. As more and more categories of goods and services become subject to the market, there are growing groups of people who cannot access what were once considered basic necessities of life. A religion that preaches good news to the poor runs up against a society that proclaims, in effect, that to be poor is to not be of value.

What we begin to see is that in some respects the market is taking on the role of a religion. In his first major writing from Rome, Pope Francis argued that "the worship of the ancient golden calf has returned in a new and ruthless guise in the idolatry of money and the dictatorship of an impersonal economy lacking a truly human purpose."[9] Likewise, Archbishop of Canterbury Justin Welby has pointed to the power of money in the world, likening it to Mammon, the financial god whom Jesus invoked.[10] Jesus may have said that one cannot serve God and Mammon but the parallels between the two today are becoming clearer. The market has its own calendar of holy days throughout the year, each designed to encourage consumption. Some of these, like Super Bowl Sunday or Black Friday, are of its own creation. But in far more instances, the market has taken over Christian holy days and directed them toward its own ends. Christmas, Easter, Halloween, and others are now primarily directed toward consumption. Instead of pilgrimages to holy sites like Canterbury or Lourdes, people now make pilgrimages to holy sites like Disneyland. Where once governments were advised by religious leaders—perhaps not the best situation for either party—they are now advised by economists with their own theologies and theories, like the rational actor, the invisible hand, or the free market.[11] A market-based society is no longer simply a tool created by humans to manage our economic interaction but a power and principality that stands in the way of abundant life for all people. It is time to begin naming it as such.

Seen in this light, Guendelsberger's inability to join her choir and attend church is not surprising. In a world where the market is like a god, people spend all their time subject to its whims and its fancies. It is an individualizing religion that militates against social activity outside the realm of economics. Perhaps the greatest challenge to Christian ministry today is simply assembling a group of people in the same place—physical or virtual—at the same time. In its voracious demand for our time and attention, a market-based society undermines precisely this activity.

What this makes clear is that while a market-based society may hide behind the guise of a value-free market, it does in fact propound values. I will return to these values in subsequent theses. To conclude this thesis, however, I want to highlight one value so engrained in the market that it functions as a kind of theology. That theology is this: in the market, what matters is what you do, and if you can't do, then you don't matter. I think of this as the Nike philosophy of life, stemming from the athletic company's longstanding slogan: Just do it. It is a seductive phrase. It tells us, first, that doing is what is important. The "just" tempts us alluringly, as if asking, What's standing in your way? Why can't you *just* do it? These finely toned athletes can: why not you? But there is good news for those of us not quite as chiseled in our physiques. What we need to do most of all, according to the reigning neoliberal ideology, is consume. Our primary identity is as consumers and this means buying more goods, using more services, and generally having more stuff. Related to this ethic of consumption is a culture that stresses performance, activity, and deed. Some families may have moved past consumption in their lives but they are still locked in frenetic patterns of activity to ensure their children get into the best possible schools, have the strongest possible college applications, and are in as strong a position as possible to succeed in the race for the diminishing number of secure jobs and houses in comfortable neighborhoods. The corollary to all of this, of course, is that if you've been unable to *just* do it, it must somehow be your own fault. A view like this leaves little room for the messy reality of human existence including our inabilities, our addictions, and our manifold human weaknesses, not to mention the full spectrum of systemic discrimination, oppression, and alienation that mark and mar our societies. The neoliberal vision of the good life—what we might call its understanding of salvation—is directly tied to human action. We are made right in the world by what we do, and this doing is often best understood as consumption. Our deeds and actions come to constitute our identity.

This vision of salvation stands in direct contrast to the theology at the heart of Christianity. In Christian theology, we are made right not by what we do but by what God in Christ has already done for us. There are many ways of understanding this action, and I will return to some of them in subsequent theses, but the important point is this: Christian theology tells us repeatedly that we are not as capable as we think we are—and that this is good news. It is good news because it is only when we recognize our imperfections that we see how God's grace and not our own actions can transform us. As Paul writes to the Romans, "I do not understand my own actions. For I do not do what I want, but I do the very thing I hate. . . . Wretched man that I am! Who will rescue me from this body of death? Thanks be to God through Jesus Christ our Lord!" (Rom. 7:15, 24–25). Christianity can have no more fundamental difference with another religion than on this question of being made right in the world—and it is on precisely this ground that the religion of the market is most different from Christianity. It propounds a theology that is antithetical to the very heart of the Christian message.

A crisis-shaped world is a world marked by the overwhelming power of a market-based society, a power that has come to function like a religion. As much as I would like it to be on some days, the Christian response is not a tear-it-all-down revolution. This is, in any event, well beyond the capabilities of most of the overstretched and overmatched Christian communities I know. Instead, Christians are called to do what they have always been called to do in response to apocalyptic powers: resist. It is a resistance that is rooted in alternate values and ways of life that challenge the debased world created by the market. It is a resistance grounded in the hope that is invoked and lived by Christians who believe God is still acting in this world. The subsequent two sections of this book explore at greater length the grounds for this resistant way of life. But first I want to explore a further aspect of the power of a market-based society.

THESIS THREE

Christian formation is not failing. It's being defeated

A clergy colleague I know was at one point in his ministry responsible for three churches. The third church was the smallest of all—just a few people hanging on at Sunday services—and the parishioners often told my colleague they felt ignored in the shared ministry. One year, he decided that to address this feeling there would be a single service on Good Friday for all three churches, and it would be held in this third church. The congregation of this third church was delighted and began making preparations.

A few days before the service, however, one of the leaders of the third church called up my colleague. "Well," he said, "you can still have the service in our church. But none of us are going to be there."

"Why not?" asked my colleague with concern.

"The local outlet mall has announced a fifty percent off sale for Good Friday and most of us have decided that we need to get to that. So we won't be able to be in church."

When my clergy colleague shared this story with me, he said that in that moment he felt a tremendous sense of failure. Here he had ministered among these people for several years and had done his best to be faithful and to share with them the good news as he understood it. In response all they could think to do was to go shopping on one of the holiest days of the year? Surely, he had done something wrong.

If you are in Christian ministry today it can be very easy to feel like a failure. Lots of very well meaning clergy and lay people are working hard to put together interesting programs, write compelling sermons, and lead engaging worship. Yet sometimes these efforts just don't seem to gain traction. People don't show up. They stare off into the middle distance distractedly, or glance at their phones too often. The ministry efforts fail in their intended purpose.

In recent decades, mainline Christians have struggled mightily to transmit their faith from one generation of believers to the next. It is this, probably more than any other factor, that is the cause of the current fragility of these churches. This struggle has given rise to a narrative among some Christians that suggests there has been a long formation failure in the church. The thinking is straightforward. Teaching and instructing people in the Christian faith is vital to forming them as Christians and passing the gospel across generations. If the gospel is not being passed across generations, then Christians must be doing a poor job of formation. If only, this line of thinking goes, we could get our act together and do formation properly, then we could ensure our Christian communities are thriving. They would come to church on Good Friday instead of heading to the outlet malls.

Part of me has long wanted to accept this argument. I work in theological education and I generally believe that more theological education of all kinds is good for the church. Still, I hesitate. I generally believe that all Christians at all times have sought to be as faithful as they could to the gospel in the best way they could discern. I also know that it is not just mainline churches that struggle to transmit their message. Immigrant and diaspora churches are confronting their own issues of generational transmission as they become more settled in their new countries. Conservative evangelical churches are increasingly struggling as well. Churches with widely differing formation practices are encountering similar issues.

The trouble with thinking that we have individually failed in ministry or that the church has collectively failed is that it places tremendous weight on human action. It is in keeping with the logic of a neoliberal, performance-driven world. But what if it is a matter not of human action but of the structures in which we find ourselves? That seemed to be the case with my colleague who lost his Good Friday congregation to the outlet mall. His congregants lived within a set of structures that made them desire low-cost goods and made those goods readily accessible through nearby outlet malls. The congregation was being formed by these structures in ways that were more powerful than any of his efforts at formation. He hadn't failed. He had been defeated.

The distinction between failure and defeat came to mind when I was a delegate to the 2023 General Synod of the Anglican Church of Canada in Calgary, Alberta. Alberta is the heartland of Canada's oil production as well as home to much of its agriculture, including cattle ranching, and Calgary is at the center of both. During the synod, members debated a resolution making worthy commitments regarding climate change, including a commitment by all parishes "to work on reducing greenhouse gas emissions." It was the kind of resolution that made abundant good sense. By the time of this meeting much of Canada and the United States had in that summer already endured weeks of intense smoke from wildfires made dramatically worse by climate change. Yet at the same time the resolution felt impotent in the face of the challenge. I was struggling with that sense of impotence when later that same day an announcement was made reminding delegates of the details of the synod's closing banquet. As befits Calgary, the banquet was to be a steak dinner held at an event venue called Gasoline Alley Museum. Given the significant carbon emissions associated with eating meat, especially red meat, and the obvious connection between petroleum products and global warming, the synod's commitments both to reducing greenhouse gas emissions and to eating steak at a museum dedicated to gasoline seemed, at best, incongruous. A friend at synod sent a tart message, "The political economy is stronger than our God."

That moment in synod—from worthy resolution to emission-producing banquet—was a moment of defeat for the church. To say this is simply to recognize that there are powers in this world that are stronger than the efforts of Christians to witness to the gospel, form people in the way of Jesus, and pass our faith from one generation to the next. That we struggle to see this in the church—that my colleague's instinctive reaction was to think he had failed with his congregation, rather than being defeated—is an indication of our inability to see with an apocalyptic clarity. But if we can reclaim that apocalyptic clarity, then the nature of the formation defeat—and the possible path forward—becomes clearer.

* * *

Implicitly or explicitly, one way to understand the goal of Christian formation is that it is to help people deepen their commitment to the gospel and the church. That prompts an important question: Why does a person change religion or make a renewed commitment to it? For many people, the answer to this question is so obvious it is rarely discussed: a person makes a decision to do so. The gospels tell us many stories of what seems to be precisely this. Jesus says to James and John to "follow him"—and they do. In the Acts of the Apostles, the early disciples are constantly preaching to and teaching people—a Roman soldier, an Ethiopian court official, a jailer—who then say, essentially, "I want to become part of this movement. Show me how." True, there is a strand of Christian theology that has emphasized God's action to predestine some people to salvation regardless of their decisions. But this has weakened in recent centuries. Instead, many people are implicitly comfortable with the words of a hymn popularized by the American evangelist Billy Graham in the twentieth century: "I have decided to follow Jesus." Following Jesus is about making an individual decision for oneself. Mainline Protestant churches today might phrase it somewhat differently—"I have decided to start attending church again"—but the emphasis is still on the decision of an individual. If we think in this way, then the formation failure argument makes sense: Christians have done a poor job of showing people why they should make the decision—and keep on making it—to follow Jesus and belong to the church.

Yet this line of thinking proceeds largely in ignorance of the considerable scholarship dedicated to religious change, conversion, and Christian adherence. What this scholarship suggests is that, contrary to popular belief, religious change is not simply a matter of individual decision. Structural factors matter as well. I was first introduced to this scholarship in the study of African Christianity where the questions of conversion and religious change are of central importance. Sub-Saharan Africa is one of the most Christian places in the world today. Yet a century or more ago, Christian missionaries struggled to interest Africans in their message. What happened to get from there to here? True, on some level millions of people decided to follow Jesus. But the scholarship suggests that these decisions were influenced by a changing set of structural conditions. As colonization, urbanization, the advent of wage labor, or civil war transformed African societies, more and more people were induced to look for new answers to the new situations they were encountering. Often, and for complex reasons, the result was Christian conversion. What looks like individual autonomy can only be understood because of the influence of the structures in which those individuals find themselves.[1]

Just as structural factors can induce people toward religious change, they can also serve as an obstacle. For instance, many pastoralist people in sub-Saharan Africa—the kind of people whose way of life centers on frequent movement in line with seasonal change—were, in the language of missionaries, "resistant" to Christian conversion for a long time. It is not that many of them were more unwilling than others to learn about Jesus. It's that their style of life meant they rarely encountered the Christian message on a sustained basis since it was confined to fixed mission stations they passed by only occasionally. The structural factor of their way of life posed an obstacle to religious change. It was only when economic, environmental, and other changes brought about a change in this style of life and pastoralist peoples began to settle in urban areas that they were exposed to the Christian message and began to consider conversion anew.[2]

Understanding the importance of structural factors in religious change does not necessarily contradict how Biblical stories of conversion have often been read. In fact, it may enhance our understanding of the Bible. While the gospels tell us about the handful of named individuals who made decisions to follow Jesus, they don't provide a clear answer for why Jesus was able to attract such massive crowds to him throughout this public ministry. For that, it may help to know something about the structure of the time in which Jesus lived. The province of Palestine was part of the vast Roman Empire. Economic changes brought about by incorporation into this empire meant that what had previously been an economy based on rural agriculture and small landowners was being transformed into an economy based on large-scale agricultural production for export on huge farms owned by absentee landowners. One result was the creation of a new and growing class of landless poor who were alienated from the economy as well as from the religious traditions of their time. These are the crowds who followed Jesus. It is not surprising that Jesus is so attentive to agriculture in his teachings, including to the reality of absentee landlords, tenant farmers, and wealthy owners who feasted while others starved (Mt. 21:33-41; Luke 16:19-31). Part of the reason Jesus' message may have been perceived as good news is that it was responsive to these changing structural conditions. No wonder so many people were interested in following him. If we can understand why the landless poor followed Jesus everywhere, we may find deeper insight into the meaning of Jesus' teachings.

When religious change is seen not simply in terms of individual decision but also in light of structure, the formation defeat idea becomes clearer. Christians are struggling to transmit their message from one generation to another because there are powerful structural forces that make it less likely for people to consider religious affiliation and church membership as a logical decision. That was what my colleague experienced when his congregation went to the outlet mall. It is in that outlet mall that we find a clue to the nature of these contemporary structural forces.

* * *

In light of the previous thesis, it should be clear that I think the dominant structural forces of a crisis-shaped world are economic. We live amid economic structures that propound a damaging and harmful set of values that are antithetical to the Christian gospel and which continue to extend their reach into ever more domains of our lives. It is hard to proclaim a gospel message that declares our salvation is not dependent on our action but on God's, while at the same time living in an environment that incessantly proclaims in implicit and explicit fashion that we are to be judged by our ability, our performance, and our deeds. It is hard to form people into an economy of giving and receiving if the dominant messages we receive are that we are to understand ourselves primarily as consumers who should find meaning through purchase and consumption. It is challenging to form people into a Christian community that meets for worship and service when labor practices of the gig economy, "side hustles," and algorithmically designed work schedules that materialize a day before they begin shred the plans of your members and prevent them from gathering together at the same time, in the same place, and on a regular basis. It is next to impossible to teach people that there are values independent of price—values like truth, love, or hope—when the market has taught us that the only value that matters is paying the lowest price of all. None of this is to make excuses for Christians and our formation practices. It is simply to say that if we are serious about the future of Christian witness, we need to think seriously not just about what we are doing but about the structural context in which we find ourselves.

Thinking about the importance of structures and their connection to Christian witness leads to an important realization: true formation is about more than just affecting someone's mind to get them to think the right thoughts. Yes, we are all shaped by what we think, but we are also shaped by desires, habits, feelings, emotions, and so much else that makes us human. If Christians are to engage in formation, then we need to engage all parts of the human person, not simply the mind. After all, Jesus told his followers to love God with all their mind, yes, but also all their heart, soul, and strength. Following Jesus engages our whole selves. Formation needs to do the same.

In a landscape shaped by rival powers to the Christian gospel, it is important to remember that Christians are not the only ones trying to form people. Other powers are as well. The Canadian theologian James K. A. Smith has been especially attuned to this. He sees the world in terms of rival liturgies. Liturgies, for him, are a "love-shaping practice" that orient our desires (or our loves) to a vision of the good life and deeper human meaning. He calls them liturgies because he is referring to practices, such as the practices that make up Christian worship services. But when Smith looks around the world, he sees lots of other liturgies. A hallmark example for him is a trip to the shopping mall. Everything from the architecture of the space, the familiar signs, brands, and symbols, the sense of escape it provides from the world outside, and the consummation of the visit in purchase suggests to him that visiting a shopping mall is a religious experience akin to the feeling a medieval pilgrim may once have had in visiting a cathedral. The liturgy of the shopping mall shapes our loves and orients us toward a vision of the good life. It's just that it is a vision of the good life that is not coherent with the Christian vision and does not ultimately lead to fullness of life. If Christians do not pay attention to both the context in which we find ourselves as well as the fullness of the person as a loving and desiring person, the result is that we could end up living in rival liturgies and "be worshipping other gods without even knowing it."[3]

Like my colleague whose congregation went to the outlet mall, there are times in my ministry when I've felt like a failure. It is a debilitating and, at times, shaming feeling. It saps energy for future efforts. It is not conducive to resisting the powers and principalities of the world. Defeat, however, is different from failure. I think about this by thinking about a sports team. Whatever the sport, by late in the season, it is clear that some teams just are not going to make the playoffs. This just isn't their year. For these teams, it can be hard to muster up the energy to get suited up and out of the locker room, let alone care about what happens on the field. These teams have failed. They have given up on themselves. But every year there are teams that work hard, practice well, and come together as a team to execute their plays—and still end up losing out on a championship. These are teams that have been defeated. As fans know, there's a world of difference between failure and defeat. There may be agony but there's no shame in playing valiantly, confidently, and well—and losing. What is problematic is being unable to even enter the arena, or playing the game so poorly you might as well never have suited up.

The Christian gospel provides the archetype of defeat: Jesus himself. When Jesus was hanging on a cross, he, his good news, and the reign of God he proclaimed sure seemed like they had been defeated. "We had hoped that he was the one to redeem Israel," two of his followers said afterward (Luke 24:21). But, the implication clearly is, he was not and did not. His kingdom had been defeated. But what Jesus on the cross was not was a failure. He had, in sports parlance, left it all on the field. He had lived confidently, spoken with authority, and confronted the powers directly, and the powers had won. But the great good news of the Christian gospel is found in precisely this: defeat is not the end. Victory is coming. Jesus was defeated but that does not mean we need to be defeatist. Quite the opposite.

Sometimes when I look—lovingly but honestly—at the church I know and care so deeply for trying its best to share its message in a crisis-shaped world, it seems like the church doesn't even know what game it is playing, let alone what arena it is taking place in. The failure to see in apocalyptic terms means we flail about. Our best efforts simply are not good enough. Not only are the powers and principalities too strong, we fail to see them and name them as such. A defeatist cynicism is not far behind. But there is another path. That path is to see with an apocalyptic clarity that names the powers and principalities that obstruct God's reign and then cultivate communities in Christ that share an ethos and set of practices that form people to live in hope, resist the powers of this world, and be a foretaste of the kingdom Jesus proclaimed and enacted. Yes, our Christian communities are fragile. Yes, the powers of this world are overwhelming in their strength. Yes, these powers shape and affect even us who proclaim that we live by the values of a different kingdom. Yes, we will almost certainly be defeated at times in our efforts to form people in the life of the reign of God. But that does not mean we have failed. It simply means that in that defeat God is waiting and working to bring forth new life in the way God has always done.

RESISTANT ETHOS

THESIS FOUR

Christians offer attentiveness to a distracted people

I did not fly often as a child. It is perhaps for that reason that the experience is firmly lodged in my memory, and especially what it was like to pass through an airline terminal in the late 1980s. There were a few shops and restaurants, the occasional television, a handful of relatively small posters advertising this or that, and some signs pointing out gate numbers, ground transportation, and arrivals and departures. Otherwise there was loads of oddly comforting industrial carpeting, plastic bucket seats, and whatever coloring books or magazines my parents had packed for me.

I travel more regularly now and of course the experience is much different. For one thing, most of that carpeting is long gone. But one of the chief ways in which it is different is the demands that traversing an airline terminal make on my attention. Terminals have been turned into shopping centers and each store wants my attention. Even if I ignore that, there are screens everywhere, some with helpful information like departure and gate information and others jammed full of ads. To make a simple journey from one gate to another or from one gate to ground transportation is to traverse an unending barrage of advertisements, announcements, images, and even scents coming from restaurants and stores, screens and signs. It is exhausting. When I finally make it to my seat on the plane, I am often confronted with another screen, this time in the seatback in front of me. This one has any number of features except for the ability to be turned off and stay off. Nor will it let me watch a movie or a safety video without serving me ads before or after.

I can't blame airports for all of this. As I pass through the airport, I carry in my pocket a device—my phone—which is tailor-made to seize my attention at every opportunity. Indeed, on the rare occasions when I find a quiet corner of an airport, my instinctive reaction is to reach for that phone and let myself be absorbed in its apps, emails, alerts, messages, and headlines. The phone has necessary information like my boarding pass or an alert about a delay. But that information is intermingled with a whole lot of other considerably less vital material only a few swipes and taps away.

My experience in an airport is just one manifestation of what is now called the attention economy. Whole business models are built on capturing our eyeballs, our senses, and our focus to sell us products and ads, or merely keep us occupied. An airport is a physical representation of this. But the attention economy is super-charged through the constant companion in the pockets of the vast majority of us who own a smartphone. The phone and its apps are designed to do everything possible to keep us logged in, engaged, and constantly scrolling and tapping. Everything from the timing of alerts to the color of displays to the frequency of sharing new information is designed to capture our attention and ensure we keep coming back for more. Keeping all of this running is "content." Whereas once content as a noun would have been plural—as in the table of contents of this book or the contents of a container—it has now become a generic, singularized product that is constantly being produced to capture and monetize our attention. There is a new profession of "content creators" whose job is the constant production of more articles, posts, images, movies, and television shows. The more of our attention we give these apps, the more the companies behind them learn about us. The more they know about us, the more they can sell that information to others for increasingly targeted ads. It works. Research varies on this but it seems that Americans check their phones something like 150 times per day. The average American spends almost four and a half hours per day on their phone or about two months per year.[1] The figures are similar in other western countries.

It might seem like an attention economy could be useful in a crisis-shaped world. After all, as a society we need to pay sustained attention to these crises. The trouble is that in an attention economy, our attention is anything but sustained. Instead, it is fractured and fragmented. Rather than being able to focus on one task or topic, the attention economy throws constant material at us that makes it impossible to focus on just one thing. I can scroll through a social media feed and see a post about someone's new job, a rant about the latest political outrage, a picture of a cat, an advertisement for something I'm never going to buy (how did that end up in my algorithm?), and a photograph of someone's most recent meal. The attention economy thrives on engagement, but it is engagement with a never-ending stream of content. The result often is not deeper engagement, but shallower.

Indeed, in recent years, a new term has become popular to describe how the attention economy intersects with a crisis-shaped world, and it is not encouraging: doom-scrolling. Doom-scrolling is the practice of continuing to scroll through bottomless social media feeds even though the content one is consuming is generally negative and depressing. The news is bad, but it has hooked our attention so deeply that we cannot stop flicking up with our thumbs. Particularly during the COVID-19 pandemic, I found myself doing this as I went to bed at night. I would check my phone to make sure the alarm was set for the right time and somehow end up on a social media feed reading one more discouraging report or damning post after another. When I checked the time, ten, fifteen, or thirty minutes would have passed. The result was that strange feeling of being both exhausted and wired at the same time. It is a feeling that is characteristic of a technology-dependent, attention-addled world.

Doom-scrolling points to the flipside of the attention economy: a growing sense of disengagement with the real challenges of the nonvirtual world and with real people in that world. It is true that social media, the hallmark of the attention economy, have been useful in bringing people together to make change. More often, however, the attention economy has encouraged us to focus on becoming unpaid content creators for social media companies who then monetize our production by selling ads back to us. This distracts our focus from the challenges facing human society in a crisis-shaped world. Pope Francis has referred to this repeatedly as the "globalization of indifference." In one representative passage he writes: "In today's world, the sense of belonging to a single human family is fading, and the dream of working together for justice and peace seems an outdated utopia. What reigns instead is a cool, comfortable and globalized indifference, born of deep disillusionment concealed behind a deceptive illusion: thinking that we are all-powerful, while failing to realize that we are all in the same boat."[2]

The challenge of a crisis-shaped world is that our attention and energy are simultaneously being seized and distracted while at the same time being directed away from the issues before a crisis-shaped world and the people that live in that world. It is a challenge not just to Christian witness but to all human society. The Christian tradition, however, has the outlines of a response.

* * *

The English word attention comes from Latin roots that mean "stretch toward." Attentiveness is about who we stretch ourselves toward. This could involve physically reaching out, but it often means where we direct our focus. Understood in this way, it becomes clear that the Christian life is in a very important way about being attentive to God. In a verse that has been important to many African Christians, the psalmist writes, "Let Ethiopia hasten to stretch out its hands to God" (Ps. 68:31). In other words, Ethiopia—and by extension Africans more generally—are called to be attentive to God. The Gospel of Mark tells of a woman with unstoppable bleeding in the crowds around Jesus. She thinks to herself that if she can reach out to Jesus and "but touch his clothes, I will be made well" (Mark 5:28). (She was right.) These passages and others are a reminder that our response to God's love is not simply a cognitive task of thinking the right thoughts but a response that engages our entire bodies. It reminds me of the ancient artwork in the Roman catacombs showing early Christians at prayer. Rather than kneeling with their hands folded together, they are standing and their hands are outstretched. (Many clergy maintain this position today while celebrating the Eucharist.) In a literal sense, the root of their prayer is a body that is attentive—stretched out—to God.

One of Jesus' most famous stories is a story about attention. In the story we call the Good Samaritan, a merchant is on his way to Jericho when he is beaten up by a gang of robbers and left to languish on the side of the road (Luke 10:25–37). A priest and a Levite—upstanding members of society who would be expected to help a distressed man—pass on the opportunity to reach out to the wounded man, instead preferring to pass by "on the other side" of the road. The third man who approaches is a Samaritan, a people who had difficult relationships with Jewish people because they were understood to stand outside the covenant God made with God's people. The listener expects the Samaritan to do the same as the priest and the Levite.

What distinguishes the Samaritan, however, is that he "came near" the merchant. He reached out to the wounded man and was attentive to him. When Jesus concludes the parable by telling his listeners to "go and do likewise," he is telling us to go show that same kind of nearness and attentiveness to others.

Many interpretations of this passage have understood the Samaritan to be a stand-in for Jesus. In the same way that the unexpected person came close to the wounded man, Jesus drew near to a people who were broken, bruised, and ignored. The attention that the Samaritan demonstrates, therefore, is an indication of the attention that is characteristic of God and God's revelation in Christ. The Incarnation of Jesus is the supreme act of God reaching out toward God's creation and, like the Samaritan, coming near to God's people: "[T]he Word became flesh and lived among us" (John 1:14). Not only does Jesus incarnate God's attention, in his ministry Jesus modeled an attention that was widespread and indiscriminate. He cared about the poor and landless people in rural Galilee, among whom he was raised and where he began his ministry. But he also was attentive to the rich and well-off, visiting their houses for meals and sharing his teachings with them. He was so popular that crowds of people gathered around him. When his disciples encouraged him not to pay attention to these crowds or tried to get them to move away, Jesus stopped them and drew those very people close. When Jesus' followers tried to send away some children, for instance, I imagine Jesus reaching out to the children and bringing them near as he said, "Let the little children come to me" (Matt. 19:14). Jesus' attention and care are a demonstration of the attention of God. God cares for the lilies of the field, which delight and inspire. So much more is God attentive to the needs and concerns of God's human creation (Matt. 6:25–33).

The language of reaching out—that is, the language of attentiveness—is made explicit in one of the prayers in the Episcopal Church's *Book of Common Prayer*. The prayer references the way in which Jesus "stretched out your arms of love on the cross," a reminder that God's attention in Christ is to the point of death. It then asks that God may "so clothe us in your Spirit that we, reaching forth our hands in love, may bring those who do not know you to the knowledge and love of you."[3] Our attention as Christians is not simply about reaching out toward God in Christ, though that is vital. If we want to be attentive to God, we also need to be attentive to one another. Jesus made this explicit when he held before his followers a vision of what is often called the final judgment. It is a vision that is rooted in attentiveness. Jesus first called those who are blessed by God into the kingdom of heaven. They are welcome because, as he said, "I was hungry and you gave me food, I was thirsty and you gave me something to drink, I was a stranger and you welcomed me, I was naked and you gave me clothing, I was sick and you took care of me, I was in prison and you visited me" (Matt. 25:34–35). These are all tasks of attention: they begin with the recognition that a person is suffering—from hunger, thirst, alienation, illness—and then respond by reaching out to that person to meet their needs. Those who are chosen to enter the kingdom do not realize that by being attentive to these people, they are actually being attentive to Jesus, but it does not change the point. Their salvation begins in their attentiveness. Likewise, for those who are not welcome, it is their failure to be attentive that is at the root of this judgment. The First Letter of John tells us that "we love because he first loved us" (1 John 4:19). Likewise, I think we can say, "we are attentive to others because God was first attentive to us."

A crisis-shaped world both shreds our attention and generates an indifference to suffering. The Christian tradition asserts that to be a human being is to be under the loving attention of God. To seek to follow in the path of Christ is to seek to live this same attention toward God and toward others in our own lives. Christian witness in a crisis-shaped world, therefore, is rooted in forming ourselves and others to place our attention in the same way Christ placed his.

* * *

It is easy to understand the stretching out of attention in a metaphorical sense. But it may make sense to think of it more literally: what position are our bodies in? I commute to work on the subway and I am frequently surrounded by people staring at their phones, locked in on the attention economy. (Indeed, I am often one of these people.) To stare at your phone has certain implications for one's body. For one thing, your hands—at least one of them—are full. It is hard to stretch out if your hands are full and drawn close to your body. There's also a posture that goes with this. The shoulders lean forward and draw in, the head and neck lean down, and the eyes are firmly fixed in the direction of the phone around one's chest. It is a posture that tends toward closure and withdrawal from the world. It is a posture that is in many ways almost diametrically opposite to stretching out, to attentiveness.

The postures I see on the subway and engage in myself remind me of how the German Reformer Martin Luther described the nature of the human condition: *incurvatus in se*. It is a Latin phrase that means "curved in upon ourselves." As he wrote in his lectures on the book of Romans: "due to original sin, our nature is so curved in upon itself at its deepest levels that it not only bends the best gifts of God toward itself in order to enjoy them. . .but it does not even know that, in this wicked, twisted, crooked way, it seeks everything, including God, only for itself."[4] The words may sound strange to our ears but they contain a basic truth. For Luther and for many other theologians, human beings are by our nature prone to focus on ourselves and seek only our own good. This is sin, and none of us escapes it. I am not aware of Luther describing it this way but another word for this might be inattentiveness. Sin prevents us from reaching out—to God, to one another, to the whole creation. The attention economy builds on that innate and metaphorical curvature to bend us, literally and figuratively, further in on ourselves so that the tendency to focus on ourselves can be monetized by others.

I am tall and always have been. When I was younger, I often found myself succumbing to the temptation many tall people feel to hunch over so as not to stick out as much. Then I went to work at a summer camp where the director was even taller than me. He pulled me aside one day and said, "Jesse, you are exactly as tall as God made you. Roll your shoulders back, stand up straight, and be who God made you to be." While I probably still slouch a bit from time to time, I've never forgotten those words. Later, I found an echo of them in the book of Ephesians: "we must grow up in every way into him who is the head, into Christ, from whom the whole body, joined and knit together by every ligament with which it is equipped, as each part is working properly, promotes the body's growth in building itself up in love" (Eph. 4:15–16). The goal of Christian life and Christian community is to continue to grow up into what Ephesians earlier describes as "maturity." We are called to keep growing, to keep stretching out, to keep rolling our shoulders back and being who God calls us to be as a Christian community. It is a community that is attentive to and reaches out to others in love and service.

When I think about growth, maturity, attention, and posture, I find myself thinking about my plot in our local community garden. There, the goal is to bring plants to maturity and reap the harvest. The growth of plants provides a real-life example of stretching out. I think of the bean seedlings that shoulder their way out of the soil just a little bent over and gradually unfurl themselves as they stretch out further. Like all plants, the beans don't want to be hunched over or curved in on themselves. They want to stretch out toward the sun and the life that it gives. My own posture in the garden mimics that of the plants. Early in the season, I am crouched down low, turning soil, making rows, and sowing seeds. As the season progresses, I come up a bit farther, weeding out undesirables, staking tomatoes or peas, and harvesting the earliest strawberries. Eventually, as the season moves toward its end, I am often standing up tall, looking around at the bounty of creation or staring at the sunflowers or amaranth that tower over even my head. Being part of the growth of the garden helps me uncurve myself. As I uncurve, I reach out and am attentive to what is happening. Early in the season, I reach out my hands to the soil to see how it has come through the winter. Later, I train vines to grow in and around other plants. I trim off stems on the tomato plants that I don't want to grow any further. Still later, I gently run my hand through the marigold and smell its distinct odor or rub my fingers on the lemon oregano and think about how it smells like lemonade. The life in the garden is one of attentiveness, and it is reflected in my posture. I look down at the soil I stand on. I look around at the plants I am growing. I look up to the sky and the rest of creation to see how my garden interacts with the weather and animals around it. It is a stretched-out, shoulders-rolled-back, uncurvedness. In my posture, it is the opposite of the attention economy.

It is the opposite in another way as well. In most cases, when I go down to the garden, I am empty-handed, save for a few tools I may need for that day's work. I go in a posture of receptivity, not knowing what may await me and what I will be given to take home with me. In contrast to the hands-full curvedness I see on the train, the garden teaches me to come empty-handed and to be attentive with those empty hands. It is an important distinction. While it is true that the Good Samaritan probably at some point had something in his hands when he reached out to the wounded man—some water, for instance, or a bandage—being attentive does not necessarily imply that we need to bring something with us. Those early Christians in the catacombs stretched out empty hands to receive from God.

There is little sign of the abating of the attention economy. Companies continue to seek our attention to sell us ads, and they do this with ever-more complex algorithms that feed us a steady diet of diverting, amusing, and incendiary content. Stretching out toward anything is awfully tough if you can just keep scrolling to the next thing. The result is a society that feels curved in on itself, with all of us walled off from one another amidst a growing sense of indifference to our crisis-shaped world and the real suffering that results. But God remains attentive to us, God's creatures, and our response to that attention remains the same as it has always been—to reach back out to God and through God to others, human and nonhuman alike. The garden offers one model of that attentiveness: uncurved, reaching out, growing to maturity, with hands empty and open to receive the goodness God is offering as we grow toward new postures of hope and mercy.

THESIS FIVE

Enough is a response to a world of more

In the second thesis, I quoted church leaders like Pope Francis who have suggested that economic structures are coming to take on the functions of a religion and acting like a god in a crisis-shaped world. This should not be a surprise. Idolatry—worshipping something that is not God—has never been far from Christianity. A market-based society, as I suggested in that earlier thesis, provides ample examples of this. This prompts a further question: what should we call this god? Jesus called this god Mammon, using a Hebrew word meaning wealth or money. In his Sermon on the Mount, he flatly said, "You cannot serve God and Mammon" (Matt. 6:24). Justin Welby, the Archbishop of Canterbury, has developed this language further, arguing that in contemporary society Mammon refers to "the power held over individuals and nations by economics, by money and flows of finance."[1]

Money is certainly powerful and its ability to distract people from the reign of God can be strong. But I think there is a deeper and more basic force at work. If I had to give a name to this god, I would call it, simply, more. In the context of the modern economy, I see this in relation to the way in which the economy is oriented toward and driven by consumption. In the wake of the Second World War and especially from the mid-1960s onwards, household spending, particularly in the United States but also elsewhere, began to grow rapidly. Before this period, the economy was more oriented around what households produced. Some households produced much of what they needed in terms of food, clothing, and shelter, leaving a smaller role for companies that produced goods for consumption. However, as the economy shifted to a post-war footing and the Baby Boom generation began to come to maturity, the advertising industry took on new prominence to generate desire and fuel continued purchases. The result was a consumer economy premised on buying the next right thing, whether it be a dishwasher, car, piece of furniture, shirts, or whatever. The economy increasingly became driven not by what people produced but by what they purchased. At a time of low inflation and growing prosperity, there was a logic to this. But beginning with the Arab oil embargo of 1973, new shocks began to make some people reconsider this economic model. The resulting inflation drove up prices and made it challenging to maintain a consumption-oriented life. By the late 1970s, American President Jimmy Carter was encouraging Americans to note how their culture had changed: "Too many of us now tend to worship self-indulgency and consumption. Human identity is no longer defined by what one does, but by what one owns. But we've discovered that owning things and consuming things does not satisfy our longing for meaning. We've learned that piling up material goods cannot fill the emptiness of lives which have no confidence or purpose."[2] Carter explicitly connected consumerism with worship to show how it was not producing meaning for people. Whatever the merits of this message and others like it, they largely went unheeded. Today, the advertising industry is an entrenched part of the landscape. It sells not just goods from ever more parts of the globe but also services, experiences, and a general quality of life that are all tied to the act of purchase.[3]

To be sure, humans do have needs that need to be met by the purchase of consumer goods and services. But a consumer-centric economy is about more than meeting these needs. It is rooted in a quest for more. The goal is not about acquiring a new pair of shoes to be well-shod. It is also about acquiring the right pair of shoes to feel good about oneself, to show off to one's friends, and now to be able to unveil them properly on social media. The same is true for the perfect vacation experience and accompanying photos. But when that moment of consumption passes, it is time to consume again and purchase something more or experience something new. Rather than focusing on what we have now, a desire for more orients us toward what comes next. Without this relentless pursuit, we are often told, the economy will sputter, and we will be unable to continue to enjoy the quality of life to which we have become accustomed.

The search for more is not only integral to a consumer economy. It is also fundamental to the broader economic model which underlies our societies. Capitalism is premised on the accumulation of profit—excess, or more—which can be reinvested to create yet more profit—more more—in an ongoing and apparently virtuous cycle. In a neoliberal era, what limits there were to the quest for more have largely been removed. That quest has resulted in corporations that now span the world as they search for more. This drives them further into places in the world that were previously out of reach, including deeper into the rainforest, farther underground, deeper under the ocean, and further into our personal lives, always searching for more: more oil, more minerals, more coal, more data. When they have found more, they need to find yet more and even more. This profit motive has been immensely beneficial in human history, resulting in new inventions, a greater spread of services, and considerable economic development. But in its current form, it is damaging and problematic for a simple reason: the world is finite. God's creation has limits. The natural world can only provide so many "resources" before it is irreparably damaged. Yet life in a neoliberal society blinds us to this recognition. In a world shaped by an ethos of more, news of the ongoing deforestation of the Amazon, for instance, large-scale data leaks, or the opening of new territory to resource exploration and extraction comes as tragic but hardly surprising news. The climate crisis is a logical culmination of the turbo-charged search for more in a finite creation.

Jesus referred to Mammon, but he also spoke about the dangers of more. At one point, he told a simple, moralistic story about a rich man whose land produced abundantly. The rich man's response was to think about more: I need more space to store all of this. Since he was a rich man, he probably already had ample space to store what he needed for the year. Yet he wanted more. But before he could enjoy the results of his new storage, he died. The point of the story is so straightforward that Jesus points to it at the beginning: "Be on your guard against all kinds of greed: for one's life does not consist in the abundance of possessions" (Luke 12:15). The Greek word Jesus uses for greed is *pleonexia*. It's a compound word: *pleon* means more and *orexis* means appetite. In this parable at least, greed is etymologically "the appetite for more." I can think of no better word to summarize the ethos of a neoliberal society. It is precisely this ethos that Jesus warns us to be on our guard against in this parable and which later on in the New Testament will be flatly equated with idolatry (Col. 3:5).

Pleonexia distorts lives by distorting our perceptions and desires. The rich man's abundance and his desire for more distorted his sense of his needs and led to misguided and foolish action. A society shaped by the drive to acquire more distorts the people who live within it. Each of us has finite amounts of energy and mental capacity to respond to the stimuli of a world directed toward more. The growing mental health crisis—anxiety, depression, loneliness—among all generations, not to mention the popularity of "self-care" are indications that many of us simply cannot handle the pressure of a world driven by more. The quest to perform, to achieve, to *just* do it one more time has become unsustainable for all of us who live in it. For those who can afford it, our consumption-oriented world has turned taking care of oneself into a further opportunity for consumption—of yoga classes, meditation retreats, vacation packages, and spas—but this only papers over the unsustainability of the path we are on.

Above all, *pleonexia* leads to a cascading series of crises, including a climate crisis driven by the appetite for more in a finite world and an economic system that entrenches inequality and misguided values in its constant pursuit of more. The COVID-19 pandemic initially seemed to prompt some people to re-evaluate aspects of their lives. But as the pandemic recedes, there is little indication on a societal level that we have given up on this constant push for more. More is a dominant, distorting, and unsustainable ethos, for the natural world and for the human beings who live in it. The Christian faith offers an alternative.

* * *

No one will ever mistake me for Keith Richards, but when I was learning to play the guitar, there was one lick I especially enjoyed playing: those first ten notes of the Rolling Stones' "(I Can't Get No) Satisfaction." They were easy and satisfying to play. I also found myself drawn to words in the first verse, a condemnation of a consumer-oriented society. The words chosen for that condemnation are telling: "more and more." This is not unfamiliar; in fact, it is the ethos of this crisis-shaped time. After this comes the song's title in its anthemic refrain: "(I Can't Get No) Satisfaction." Like *pleonexia,* "satisfaction" is a compound and etymologically rich word. Its Latin roots are *satis* meaning "enough" and *faction* from the word that means "to make or do." Satisfaction is, literally, to do enough. In a world governed by more, the Rolling Stones recognize that it is precisely satisfaction that we can't get. In an advertising-driven, consumer-oriented society, we will never have enough. We will always need the next purchase. A corporation will never be satisfied with the amount of oil it has in reserve or the amount of data it holds on us because it is oriented to constantly acquire more to expand its profit and grow further still.

There is a moment in Exodus that highlights the difference between more and enough. When God's people were slaves in Egypt, one of their jobs had been to build storage facilities for all of Pharaoh's grain (Exod. 1:11). Pharaoh's kingdom and economy were structured around control of grain and he could never have enough or be satisfied. He always needed more, and he needed more storage to accommodate it all. It is not all that different from the rich man about whom Jesus would later tell his followers. It was, in part, to free the people from this burden of producing more for Pharaoh that God sent Moses to Egypt to lead God's people out of slavery. But once Moses and the people left behind Pharaoh and his armies and set out across the wilderness, they got hungry. In response, God offered them a strange flakey substance that was so unusual they called it "What is it?" or in Hebrew *manna*. But manna was governed by an important principle: they must only "gather enough for that day" (Exod. 16:4) and not store any up for tomorrow, except for the day before the sabbath when they could take twice as much. Inevitably, some of the people did not listen and took extra. Who can blame them? They had just escaped slavery and were traveling in the wilderness with uncertain prospects for more food. But the extra they took gets consumed by worms and they learn a lesson about enoughness. They were to take "as much as each needed," but not more than that (Exod. 16:21). The reason is clear: if they stored up food for the future, they were little different from Pharaoh and his grain towers. But by only taking enough for one day, they were learning about the difference between the way of life God was calling them to and the way of life in the economy they left behind: don't think about more; concentrate on enough.[4]

I have had an echo of this feeling of enoughness in my own food practices. The pandemic accelerated a practice I began in the years leading up to it of preserving and canning food for my family. I've figured out now how much I need to make to see my family through a year and have some left over to give to friends: fifteen pints of jam, twelve quarts of salsa, and forty quarts of applesauce. When I reach those numbers (give or take a couple), I know that I have done enough. I also know that that is about all my family and work schedule will allow for. I'd like to store some pickles, for instance, or can peaches or other fruit, but I know I don't have enough time to do this. So I trade with friends, go without, or buy them at the store. I try to be honest about my limits as well as the limits of what my family can actually consume. When I count up my jars in the closet and realize I've reached my numbers, I store my canning equipment at the back of the cupboard for another year with a feeling of satisfaction. I have done enough. For me, it is a feeling of peace that is a life-giving contrast to a world of more.

Satisfaction is used in Christian theology in relation to Jesus Christ. The Anglican prayer book tradition has given us the phrase "a full, perfect, and sufficient sacrifice, oblation, and satisfaction" in reference to Christ's work on the cross.[5] Jesus' death is a satisfaction. Without venturing too far into the theology of atonement, I want to note this: the phrase is a reminder that the principles of God are principles of enoughness. God and Jesus teach us to be satisfied and not be consumed by an appetite for more. But not only do they teach us this. Ultimately, Jesus in his life, death, and resurrection does enough for our salvation. Nothing else—not by Jesus, not by us, not by anyone else—needs to be done for us to be right with the world and feel we have done enough.

Other authors in the Bible also recognized the damage that could be caused by the quest for more. In describing the fall of Babylon/Rome in Revelation, John pays particular attention to "the merchants of the earth" whom he sees weeping and in mourning "since no one buys their cargo anymore." He offers a lengthy list of the luxury goods and staples of upper-class life that people no longer buy. "Alas, alas," the merchants cry out, "in one hour all this wealth has been laid waste!" (Rev. 18:11–17) The return of Christ brings an end to a consumer economy premised on more. However, as the parable of the rich man and his storage indicates, it is not an easy message to internalize. If our economic structures or relationship with creation are any indication, it is a message we do not understand either.

I have often wondered if the church doesn't understand the message of enoughness either. At this time of great change, there is increasing pressure on clergy and lay leaders to do more, be more, and try more, as if with just a little bit of extra effort, we could unlock the key to future transformation. With fewer people coming to church, there is increasing pressure on those remaining to do more to maintain some vision of what the church once was. Many people are trying to sustain a vision of the church's ministry bequeathed to us by a previous generation. Sometimes it seems the only way to do this is if we constantly work ourselves to the bone. In our messaging, the church communicates this desperation for more. We need more volunteers! We need more people in church! We need more people at this upcoming event! But instead of offering an escape from the damaging ethos of the world and being a site of resistance to the anxious search for more, these strategies simply manifest and perpetuate it, albeit cloaked in church-based language. The church can sometimes be a place where it is all too easy to sing, "(I Can't Get No) Satisfaction." That is, "I can't do enough." The result is the feeling of failure and defeatism I described in a previous thesis.

An ethos of more is unsustainable and damaging—to Creation, to our relationships with one another, to ourselves, and to our church.

God gives us enough and through Christ has done enough. We already have what we need to love and serve God in God's world. We do not need more.

* * *

There is a final word that helps me think about the place that more plays in our world, and I introduced it in the previous chapter: content. Ask yourself how you read "content" just now because it is a funny word. If you place the emphasis on the first syllable—CON-tent—it is a noun and refers to what an attention economy encourages us to focus on. The success or failure of each piece of content can be measured with statistics about hits, views, and engagements. Whatever the metric, the number is never high enough. More engagement is always needed. Content, in this sense, is at the center of an economy premised on the search for more. However, if you place the emphasis on the second syllable—con-TENT—it is an adjective that means something like peacefulness or settledness. In my mind, content and its related noun contentment are synonyms for satisfied. When we are content with something, we are at peace with the way things are and do not need more.

Content may be everywhere, but contentment remains out of reach for growing numbers of people. The rigors and disciplines of a market-based society mean that having enough for survival is becoming unattainable for many. Social media and technology more generally fuel a constant sense of comparison that leaves many people feeling dissatisfied and left out. The impacts of this loss of contentment are manifold, ranging from the growing mental health crisis to an unhealthy populist political movement. The American way of life is famously rooted in "life, liberty, and the pursuit of happiness." But a lot of people in the United States and in the many countries influenced by its politics, culture, and economy, do not seem very happy.

The funny thing about happiness is that it is a hard thing to have. The reason is that happiness is often measured, at least implicitly, in relative terms. I can only be happy if I have more than, say, my neighbor or if I have just a bit more money than I have now. Happiness, through the consumer culture in which we live, also comes through acquisition—not so much possession, but buying the next thing. But that is the ethos of more and we have already seen that it is a dead end. Still, popular depictions of the good life persist in demonstrating how it relies on something more than what we don't have right now.

Instead of happiness, Christian witness is rooted in contentment. Contentment does not rely on comparison. It relies instead on an informed judgment of what makes for peace and enoughness. Instead of going along with a society that insists on happiness and more, Christian communities need to discover themselves anew as places of satisfaction and contentment. The gospel offers not simply words of exhortation—do more already!—but also of consolation—come to me and rest. The Christian community is the place where we do not—should not—need to do more to prove we belong. It is the place where those made weary by the struggle to survive can find rest and refreshment. In a world of more, enough, satisfaction, and contentment are powerfully consoling words.

It is challenging for Christian communities to be places of consolation when the ethos of more has already taken such deep root, including in our very communities. It is even harder to think about moving our societies to places of contentment when so many people struggle to have enough to live, survive, and be content. It will take a robust set of spiritual practices to say enough to a world defined by *pleonexia*. This is a theme I will return to in upcoming theses. Nonetheless, our living as Christians can begin by being grounded in the knowledge of the enoughness of God. God gives us enough. God in Christ has done enough. Each one of us is enough. That is good news. And it can be a source of satisfaction for a world dying from its love for more.

THESIS SIX

The catholicity of the Christian community is its response to a globally-connected world

I have already suggested that I grew to adulthood in what in retrospect seems like a charmed time. The Cold War was over, the peace dividend was being reaped, politics were stable, inflation was low, and the stock market was booming. To describe this new era that succeeded the end of nuclear power competition and divided blocs confronting one another, commentators settled on a new word: globalization. It seemed apt. Thanks to both technological and policy changes, the world was becoming more connected. More and more people were becoming aware of being part of a global community and were benefitting from their connection to it. Whether it was international airline travel, shipping routes that sent finished goods around the world, internet connections that allowed for near-instant communication, or any of a number of other developments, many—but by no means all—people around the world were led into deeper relationships with one another. We might not always have been aware of these relationships but it was no longer uncommon to have clothes made in some far distant country or use technology manufactured elsewhere and shipped to us where we were. As these examples suggest, many of these global relationships were oriented around the market and the economy. Globalization was a close relation of the neoliberal economic model that was becoming settled consensus. Initially, the advent of globalization was seen as a largely positive development. Growing trade and communication links put more people in touch with one another, facilitated economic growth, and improved the standard of living.

Globalization looms large in my imagination because it reached a kind of peak as I was in university and entering into greater political and economic awareness. The accession of China to membership in the World Trade Organization in 2001 brought China more fully into the global economy and allowed it to become a "workshop for the world." This move remains a high-water mark of the period in which globalization was seen in a largely positive light. But that view was beginning to change. In 1999, not long before China's accession, protests at the annual meeting of the WTO turned violent and became known as "The Battle for Seattle." Two years later, leaders from across North and South America came together in Quebec City for what they called the Summit of the Americas. Their goal was to make progress on a free trade agreement spanning the two continents. It was the major political event on the calendar that spring and attracted significant media attention. A friend and I attended a weekend teach-in at our university where we learned about the difference between free trade and what was called "fair trade." We also sat together on the floor and learned the techniques of nonviolent civil disobedience and what to do if we were arrested. In the end, we never went to Quebec City, but I remember the energy around the event and the attention it commanded. Even as China's membership in the WTO offered a symbolic marker of the consensus about globalization, there was also significant concern that the drawbacks of globalization were not being properly taken into account. The neoliberal consensus around free trade did not seem to properly account for those who would suffer from this decision. In the push to move forward, those concerns risked being forgotten.

Global interconnectivity wasn't just about economic relations, however. Many people learned this in particularly acute fashion on September 11, 2001. The response to the terrorist attacks on the

United States that day was branded a "global war on terror," but against whom was it to be directed? Wars were meant to be fought between nation states. Yet here was a war initially directed against terrorists who did not represent any particular nation but rather embodied a cause and an ideology. They were able to use the tools of a global world—air travel, communications, technology—to launch an unprecedented attack. Even as global interconnectivity deepened, it was becoming clear that the benefits of this interconnectivity were not universal.

In the more than two decades since my university days, the discourse and activity surrounding globalization have changed. But our global interconnectivity has only grown. The COVID-19 pandemic spread around the world with such speed precisely because of our global connections. But it does not take a pandemic to see global connectivity. I wrote this book on a computer designed in California, manufactured in China with parts and materials from around the world, and sold to me in Montreal. I refreshed my memory about the date of the Quebec City meeting with some Internet research made possible by routers, modems, and other equipment that is similarly designed in one part of the world, manufactured in another, operated in a third, and which bring information to me regardless of where I sit in the world.

The truth is I've been a beneficiary of our interconnected world. Since graduating from university, I've taken advantage of the ease of international travel to travel and live in countries around the world and learn about different cultures, contexts, and churches. My horizons have been expanded and I think in new ways about what is considered "normal" and about how different societies approach the challenges we all face. Today, I live in a city that is one of the most multicultural in Canada. My neighbors are from the Ivory Coast, Algeria, and Hungary, as well as Canada. The theological college I lead and the university where I teach have students from across the globe. I use modern communication tools that mean I can be in touch with someone across the world almost as easily as I can with someone down the hall from my office. The clothes I wear, the food I eat, and the technology I rely on all show evidence of the global influences that shape my life.

But increased global interconnectivity has not been equally good for everyone. People at the Battle for Seattle and the Summit for the Americas spotted this with their concerns about fair trade. That rhetoric has now been joined by opposition from different points on the political spectrum. Politicians have risen to prominence who oppose global connections and are concerned about the loss of state sovereignty, the economic impacts of trade agreements, and the vanishing manufacturing industry in their countries. The debate during the Brexit referendum of 2016 followed these lines. Opponents of membership in the European Union were protesting the way in which they thought that membership disadvantaged the United Kingdom. They combined concern with rising rates of immigration with more nebulous appeals to concepts like sovereignty and the desire to "take back control." Support for Donald Trump's presidential campaign in 2016 was strong in areas of the United States that have been particularly hard-hit by the decline of manufacturing and other economic changes associated with globalization.

At the heart of globalization is a tension between the local and the universal. Globalization brings together a local particularity and a universalizing norm. Sometimes this is positive. The universalizing norm of common Internet and email standards, for instance, brings together my local situation with that of others around the world. At other times it can unsettle. The universalizing norm of the free movement of people in the European Union sat uncomfortably with the sense of uncontrolled change that many people felt in communities across England. As countries became more closely tied to one another through international trade, the integration of global supply routes and chains of production became increasingly important, even as it has led to the decline of local economies dependent on manufacturing. Part of the opposition to globalization has been rooted in the way in which these universalizing forces sit uneasily with the shuttered factories in communities that were once centered on them.

As I've experienced it, for much of the last twenty years the answer that the world has provided to this tension between universalizing norm and local particularity has been basically this: get over it. Think of yourself as a consumer first and enjoy cheap clothes, cheap food, and fancy technology at low cost. Don't you understand that this system is the most efficient—and therefore best—way to structure our society? For much of the time, there has been little meaningful engagement with those who cannot find their way in this evermore interconnected world. Globalization is the way it needs to be. But Brexit, the presidency of Donald Trump, and the rise of similar populist leaders reaffirms what should have long been obvious: not everyone is on board the globalization express.

Initially, it seemed possible that the pandemic would undo some of the forces of global integration. Travel was curtailed and there was new concern about how some products, like medical equipment, were sourced. But with the pandemic fading into memory, this seems increasingly unlikely. Global travel demand is bouncing back. Some countries, led by the United States, are trying to bring economic production closer to home and may succeed for certain products. These will likely be exceptions that prove the rule. The reliance of our dominant economic model on ever-expanding markets and ever-lower costs means globalization will continue to be part of our lives. Moreover, regardless of any deliberate efforts, the technology of our world is such that universalizing forces and local contexts will continue to be brought together. The result may not be another pandemic but may be continued political and economic tension over the locus of power and the future of human communities. If economic globalization is not the answer, we still need to find a way to have these encounters between global and local. For me, that answer lies in a word with deep roots in the Christian tradition: catholic.

* * *

Catholic can be a misleading word. My father grew up in a Lutheran church that recited the Apostles' Creed on Sundays. But they made one change. Rather than affirm the line, "I believe in. . .the holy catholic church," they said they believed in "the holy Christian church." For a church that was constituted through its break with Roman Catholicism, the historic affirmation was a step too far. But the congregation was making a mistake. It was mixing up what you might call big-c Catholic—the name of a church—and little-c catholic. It's that latter word that is of interest to me.

Catholic is often translated as "universal." This is one way of rendering its Greek root words that mean literally "in respect of the whole." When we say that catholic means universal we are also saying something like "related to wholeness." Wholeness itself is an idea that pervades the Judeo-Christian tradition. The Hebrew word *shalom* runs throughout the Old Testament and is often translated as peace. But a more accurate translation might be "wholeness" in reference to the full and complete relationships that God creates with and among God's people. It is this idea that Jesus is drawing on when he teaches his followers to "be perfect, therefore, as your heavenly father is perfect" (Matt. 5:48). "Perfect" here means something similar to wholeness and completeness. Catholic stands in this tradition and is a reminder that God acts to create wholeness for God's people.

Catholic is such an important word that Christians have made it one of the four fundamental affirmations of the church: the Nicene Creed declares the church to be one, holy, catholic, and apostolic.

Historically, the affirmation that the church is catholic has been interpreted in a couple of different fashions. Most simply, the catholic church is a universal church in the sense that it is present around the world. That is something I've learned and re-learned as I've taken advantage of the travel links of our globalized world to visit far-off places and always find Christians at the end of the journey. But even on the day of Pentecost, the "birthday of the church" when the followers of Jesus were in Jerusalem, the church was catholic. The catholicity of the church is not simply about its extent but about the comprehensiveness of its teaching and the salvation it offers. The fourth-century theologian Cyril of Jerusalem wrote:

> The Church is called Catholic because it is spread over all the world, from one end of the earth to the other; and because it teaches universally and completely one and all the doctrines which ought to come to men's knowledge, concerning things both visible and invisible, heavenly and earthly; and because it subjects to right worship the whole race of mankind, governors and governed, learned and unlearned; and because it universally treats and heals the whole class of sins, which are committed by soul or body, and possesses in itself every form of virtue which is named, both in deeds and words, and in every kind of spiritual gifts.[1]

To affirm that the church is catholic is to affirm both that the gospel teaches people all they need to know and is for all people.

In a globalized world, catholic takes on new salience and significance. To understand why, it is important to see the parallels between the dynamics of globalization and the dynamics at the heart of the Christian gospel. Globalization is about a tension between the local and universal. So, too, is the Christian gospel. On the one hand, Jesus Christ is the incarnate son of God whose good news is for all people everywhere. That's why he tells his followers to take his good news to the ends of the earth and why the church has, in the centuries since, spread across the world. The Christian gospel has a universal scope. But the foundation of that gospel is a set of events—birth, life, death, resurrection—that took place at a particular moment in a particular place: Palestine under Roman occupation two thousand years ago. In the interplay between those unique events and their universalizing impetus is found the gospel of Christ.

This tension between the particular and the universal has cropped up often in the life of the church. The Bible is suffused with agrarian imagery and metaphors like seeds, planting, and mustard bushes. But how do hunter-gatherer societies understand this? Feminist theologians have asked how the particular fact of Jesus' maleness influences their understanding of the universal message of salvation: can a male Messiah save women? Peter, Paul, and other early Christian missionaries encountered a similar difficulty. The first Christians were Jewish and thought nothing of following the Jewish dietary laws and practicing male circumcision. These were particular practices that made sense to them. But the universalizing force of the gospel brought them into contact with people who wanted to follow Jesus but were not Jewish: did they have to follow the dietary laws and be circumcised? The New Testament tells us that it wasn't an easy question to answer but the answer, ultimately, was no. It was possible to follow the universalizing impetus of the Christian gospel but leave behind local particularities associated with its expression.

The comparison of globalization and catholicity reveals an important difference. The tendency of globalization is toward homogenization. The more that consumers around the world can be the same and want the same things, the easier it is for globe-spanning corporations to serve us. That's why, for instance, an important part of globalization has been the growth of multinational corporations like Coca-Cola or McDonald's. An Indonesian in Jakarta and an

American in Jacksonville can both be served the same hamburger and fries. While it is true that these corporations make some concessions to local realities—no hamburgers in India, for instance—most aim for the greatest similarity possible between their products wherever in the world they may be consumed. The more that people around the world are the "same kind" (a literal meaning of homogenous), the easier it is for us to be seen as undifferentiated consumers of products in a global world.

But this homogenization across the richness of global diversity is false. We need look no further than the church to see this. Across time and place, churches have been shaped by the cultures in which they find themselves. Compare the worship of Russian Orthodoxy to American evangelicalism, for instance, or the theology of the Church of England with that of the Coptic Church in Egypt. Yes, there are similarities but it is the differences that immediately make an impression. Yet all are part of the same catholic church. The same is true for global human society. Cultures shape values and expressions of life in ways that can seem impossible to reconcile. This doesn't mean that we withhold judgment or keep to ourselves. But it does mean that when we engage with people from around the world, the proper first step is to recognize where they are coming from and what they bring with them. Heterogeneity is of deep value to Christians. To be sure, the church has failed at this many times in its history. When Christians from the North Atlantic world have encountered people from other cultures—a process called mission—there has been a strong tendency to want to homogenize into a single model of Christian. The result was, for instance, residential schools that sought to strip students of their culture to "save" them or missionaries who went to Africa seeking to bring "commerce, Christianity, and civilization," not understanding that it is possible to follow Jesus without also adopting western styles of dress, education, and economics. Imperialism, colonialism, and racism have compromised and compromise today the church's affirmation of its own catholicity.

The way globalization resolves the tension between global and local is, as I have said, to have the former steamroll the latter. A single set of global norms is, in an ideal globalized world, meant to structure all interactions and result in low-cost consumption. But the answer the Christian tradition provides is, at its best, somewhat more nuanced. The Christian tradition envisions higher goods than convenient consumption. It does this by affirming the catholicity of Christianity. This affirmation values both the global and universal on the one hand and the local and particular on the other. Rather than prize an undifferentiated and homogenized uniformity, the catholic church embraces a glorious, often messy, heterogenous unity. Rowan Williams, the former Archbishop of Canterbury, described it this way:

> The catholic is the opposite of the globalized, because the catholic is about wholeness, about the wholeness of the person, the wholeness of local culture and language. Therefore it's not simply opening the same fast-food shop in every village on the globe, and it's not like the global economy, in which people are drawn into somebody's story and somebody's interests which in fact makes others poor and excluded. The catholic is the opposite of the globalized because the catholic is about everyone's welfare, everyone's growth and justice.[2]

The way in which the gospel is expressed in one context may be different from the way it is expressed in another context. But there is a universal tie that binds them together. Recognizing and deepening that tie is the calling of a catholic church.

In my theological imagination, I associate catholic with wholeness, unity, and, of course, the church. These words bring me to another phrase: body of Christ. Central to the New Testament understanding of the Christian community is the idea that to fully follow Christ, we need other Christians. We need to give gifts to the community and receive from others. When I think about the church in this light, I am reminded that the catholicity of the church is not simply an interesting feature of Christian life to affirm in the creed. It is, rather, essential to my own ability to follow in the way of Jesus. I've been reminded of this countless times when I've made advantage of our global interconnectedness to meet Christians from other contexts. When I've worshipped with Indigenous Christians in northern Canada, I've learned about how their faith is tied to their relationship with the land—and wondered how I am called to relate to God's creation in my urban environment. When I've worked with South Sudanese Christians who are working to build a peaceful country, I've learned about how Christians are called to be active in the public and political spheres where they find themselves—and wondered how I am called to do the same in my own context. The tensions and challenges posed by a catholic church are not always easily resolved or answered. Seeking the unity of a catholic church rather than the uniformity and homogeneity of a globalized world is necessary, but not easy.

Global interconnectivity is not going away. The technologies we have created will continue to bring local contexts across the world into contact with universalizing forces. Experience demonstrates that particularly in economic realms the logic of globalization is toward uniformity. As the political turmoil of recent years has demonstrated, few people are satisfied with this logic. This is an opportunity for Christians to affirm the catholicity of our communities in new ways. Mindful of our own challenging history, this call to catholicity is also a call to repentance for the ongoing entanglement of Christians—especially those from racially and economically privileged backgrounds—in homogenizing forces in the world. With this in mind, Christians who affirm catholicity have an opportunity to show the world how the tension between local and global, particular and universal can be not only managed but turned into a place of flourishing. God calls all people to wholeness and Christ's church is meant to embody this wholeness and universality as a gift to the world. When we remember this, we can truly affirm that we are catholic Christians and offer good news to a global world.

THESIS SEVEN

In an angry world, the Christian answer is mercy

During the COVID-19 pandemic, our college needed a new credit card. Dealing with banks and their stringent know-your-customer requirements is not my idea of a good time but it turned out that I was the only one who was able to open this account. I gritted my teeth and picked up the phone. I expected the usual run-around through various telephone chains and that is what I got: contradictory and unclear information, a promise to send information right away and then nothing further, and staff who didn't seem aware of the bank's own policies posted on their websites. Although this kind of bureaucracy is frustrating and time-wasting, I have, in the past, usually been able to maintain my composure and be polite to the person on the other end of the phone. After all, I reason, they're only a cog in a machine and they're human just like me.

But this time was different. As I worked my way through the various extensions and people, I found myself getting angrier and more upset than usual. Finally, I found myself loudly raising my voice with a young man on the other end of the line who—and I simply could not believe this—could not open a new account for me, even though three other people had directed me to this extension and I had provided all the information the bank requested. When I hung up the phone—without having secured a new credit card—I was embarrassed and abashed at the encounter. That night at the subway station I spotted a sign in the window of the information desk that said, "Reminder: Be kind, be respectful. Bullying, harassment, and aggressive behaviour towards staff, or others, will not be tolerated." Rarely have I felt so directly addressed by a generic public notice. My ride home that evening was in a spirit of chastisement.

Signs like these have become more common in many public places like businesses or government offices. Sometimes they are couched, like the one I saw, as reminders. Other times they are more direct: "Physical and verbal violence against our staff will not be tolerated." The pandemic was a turning point for these signs. You only had to read the news to understand why. The pandemic provided numerous stories of front-line employees who had been forced to deal with the brunt of a customer's rage: airline attendants who asked passengers to properly wear masks or store employees who asked people to maintain appropriate physical distancing. When Quebec implemented a vaccination passport that required customers to show proof of vaccination before entering big box stores, several store owners publicly expressed concern about the abuse their employees might suffer as a result of having to enforce it.

The pandemic was a moment of significant societal-wide stress. Everyone, virtually without exception, endured pressure on our normal routines. Some people, notably health care workers and other essential workers, endured profound and unrelenting pressure. But it is not just the pandemic. In a crisis-shaped world pressure comes from multiple directions at once. For many people in the world, living under stress and pressure is not new. But for people who come from backgrounds like mine, a crisis-shaped world is making it clear that our privilege cannot protect us from this stress and pressure. It can come from concern about the future direction of climate change. It can come from fear about not having enough money to make it to the next paycheck and the financial precarity and economic uncertainty that attends more and more lives. It can come from the sense of loss that can be attached to witnessing the transformation of neighborhoods by new arrivals. It can come from the fear of having to enforce an unpopular vaccination passport or from being a new immigrant in a suspicious community. Sometimes these pressures find healthy outlets, such as the new exercise routines or new relationship with one's work that the pandemic brought about for some people. Other times, these outlets are much less healthy and include getting upset, or much worse, with employees who bear no blame for a situation. The pressure of living in a crisis-shaped world is pushing many people toward greater upset, anger, and rage.

* * *

I grew up in the 1980s and 1990s, which means I was of an age to be a prime target for the Walt Disney Company's successful launch of animated musical movies. Almost every year like clockwork, there was a new feature film, usually around the end of the year, featuring singing lobsters, lions, candlesticks, or whatever. First, "The Little Mermaid" in 1989, then "Beauty and the Beast" in 1991, "Aladdin" in 1992, and the "Lion King" in 1994. Each had an all-encompassing promotional strategy and songs written by some of the most talented musicians in the world. It worked. Those lyrics are still imprinted on my brain three decades later.

These movies shared something else in common as well. Each of the climactic scenes featured an intense battle and struggle between the hero(s) of the movie and their antagonists. The climax of "The Little Mermaid" features Prince Eric facing off against the gigantic sea witch, Ursula. Eric defeats Ursula by ramming a ship into her abdomen and sending her to the bottom of the ocean. In "Beauty and the Beast," the Beast fights the louche anti-hero Gaston across the ramparts of a castle before Gaston plummets to his death. In "Aladdin," the evil Jafar seems to be about to triumph and take control of the kingdom of Agrabah before plucky Aladdin taunts him in such a way that Jafar ends up trapped in a lamp. In the

"Lion King," Simba returns to his kingdom to defeat his usurping uncle Scar in a battle royale that involves hyenas, lionesses, a wise old baboon, a warthog, and a meerkat. The logic of these endings is taken for granted. The movies have set up opposition between good and evil, protagonist and antagonist, hero and villain. In mass-market popular culture, there is only one way these stories can end: the triumph of good and, just as importantly, the defeat of evil. Evil has done wrong, whether in usurping a throne, attacking a castle, or seeking to rule the ocean, and the only way for that wrong to be punished is for it to be comprehensively and utterly defeated to the point of death, or, barring that, an eternity trapped in a magic lamp. This logic is often obscured by turning these battles to the death into humorous moments—that's what the warthog and meerkat are for—but its outlines are clear.

The theologian Walter Wink coined the phrase "the myth of redemptive violence," which means what it sounds like. Redemptive violence is the belief that violence can set situations right. The Disney movies that were so formative for my generation are steeped in this idea. Each sets up a wrong that is only righted by the climactic battle. No other option is presented: it is only by violence that wrongs can be overturned. (They also demonstrate how redemptive violence is a highly gendered idea: it is the male characters who are called to lead the quest for redemption through violence.) However, Wink rightly points out that violence does not fix problems. It creates new ones. Wink demonstrates how Jesus offers a different model. Jesus did not use violence to bring in his kingdom, even though some of his followers wanted him to. Instead, Jesus allowed himself to be the victim of violence and, through this, established a new kingdom rooted in peace. Redemption through violence, Wink says, is a myth, but it is one that is deeply rooted in western culture. It is also one taught to our children, including me, from a very young age.[1]

I first learned about the myth of redemptive violence many years ago. Yet that did not stop me from yelling down the phone line at a bank agent. On some level, I was convinced that if I could just unload my frustration on someone, my problem would be solved. Or, if the problem was not solved, I might at least feel better. It made me wonder if the pandemic and the broader societal stresses of this moment in history are not making many people more open to the myth of redemptive violence. Certainly the crises of our moment, including the pandemic, are making many people feel a sense of loss. Again, this is especially true for people like me in relatively privileged positions in society who are accustomed to making plans, getting our way, and having the pieces fall into place. But a crisis-shaped world can suddenly upend plans for a vacation or a family reunion, as has happened to me. During the pandemic, my privilege did not spare me, and all of us, from losing time I will never get back. While many people throughout history have long known this, the crises of this moment are making many more people realize that we are not as isolated or safe as we once thought we might be. Viral transmission, forest fires, superstorms, and heat domes can come for us as well.

The result is that people who are used to having things work out are left seeking some kind of redemption or restoration. The trouble is that since what we are losing in a crisis-shaped world isn't any one person's fault—it's the fault of a virus, maybe, or our collective actions and inaction—then we don't really know who to blame. But front-line staff are most visible and become easy targets. I was not really upset about how hard it was to open a new business credit card account (though I have some good ideas on how to simplify the process). Rather, I just could not handle this additional pressure in a life that felt already overburdened. I lashed out at the easiest target, the person on the other end of the phone. But this did not redeem the situation or make things right. It did not get me any closer to getting a credit card. What would?

* * *

At the beginning of his public ministry, Jesus returned to the synagogue in his hometown of Nazareth. He was given the scroll of the prophet Isaiah to read, stood up, and offered what has sometimes been called his inaugural address. He read, "The Spirit of the Lord is upon me, because he has anointed me to bring good news to the poor. He has sent me to proclaim release to the captives and recovery of sight to the blind, to let the oppressed go free, to proclaim the year of the Lord's favor" (Luke 4:18–19). Jesus was quoting from Isaiah 61 but he made one major edit to the original text. The Isaiah passage says that the messenger is to "proclaim the year of the Lord's favour, and the day of vengeance of our God" (Isa. 61:2). Jesus read the part about proclaiming the year of the Lord's favor—and then was entirely silent about the day of God's vengeance. I cannot imagine this was a mistake. Jesus was a precocious child in the temple who taught religious elders about their faith. He knew his stuff. He did not accidentally leave off a part of the verse. It was a deliberate omission meant to tell us something about Jesus and the shape of his ministry.

Given how the story turns out, Jesus' omission of vengeance is somewhat ironic. After Jesus concluded his reading, he suggested to his hearers in Nazareth that God's promises extend beyond the Jewish people. He reminded them of how the prophet Elijah was sent during a famine not to a Jewish household but to a Gentile one to help. This enraged those in the synagogue with him. They drove him out of town to the edge of a hill to hurl him to his death. But he passed through them and went on his way. Something about what Jesus had done offended the sensibilities of the people in Nazareth. Perhaps it was that Jesus omitted a reference to vengeance. Perhaps it was that he suggested that people who seem undeserving are within the love of God. Whatever it was, a story that begins by omitting vengeance concludes with Jesus' listeners in a rage.

In his ministry, Jesus enacted what he proclaimed in his inaugural address. He shared good news with the poor. He set free those who were captive to sin and disease. He healed. He fed. And he repudiated rage and vengeance. There were certainly those among Jesus' followers who wanted him to seek vengeance. Not long after the visit to the synagogue in Nazareth, Jesus and his followers happened to pass through a Samaritan village. A couple of his apostles asked if they should rain down fire and destroy this village of people who historically had strained relations with Jesus' Jewish people (Luke 9:51–56). Not only did Jesus rebuke them for this, almost immediately afterward he told one of his most famous stories, that of the Good Samaritan. A representative of this despised people could be a vehicle of the love that was the center of Jesus' ministry. In its timing, the story serves as an implicit reminder that even in relation to those people against whom we seek vengeance, another way might be possible.

Most of all, Jesus lived at a time in which many people yearned for political liberation from the oppressive rule of the Roman Empire and its client king. There were those who were convinced that the only way forward was a military revolution and the overthrow of the oppressors. Jesus did not endorse this way either. Instead, Jesus was crucified and, for a time, the hopes of his followers died with him. When Jesus was raised again, he came back to his followers. If ever there was a moment when there was a clear right and a clear wrong, this was it. Here was a man unjustly put to death and raised from the dead. It was time for vengeance. Yet when Jesus returns, he says, "Peace be with you." He breathes the Spirit on his followers and sends them out into the world in that same spirit—not a spirit of vengeance but a spirit of peace (John 20:21-22). Redemptive violence is, indeed, a myth.

* * *

There's a word that describes our desire for things to be set aright, and it is found at the end of the arc of the moral universe: justice. Justice is deeply rooted in western philosophy and politics, and it has numerous definitions. One of the most consistently influential views of justice originates with the ancient Greeks, who spoke of justice as giving to each what is his or her due. The endings of those Disney movies can be interpreted as just because the evil anti-heroes receive what is their due, namely death and destruction, while the heroic good guys also are restored to their due, namely power and glory. The logic is not all that different from the logic of the classic western movie: there are good guys on the side of the law and bad guys outside the law. The good guys deliver justice by defeating the bad guys. It is this same desire for justice, for setting things aright, that lies at the root of much of the rage in society today. I felt wronged by the service I received from the bank in opening a new account. I lashed out at the person it was easiest to lash out against in a—futile—effort to correct this wrong and receive what I thought was due to me.

To be sure, justice is used in more expansive fashions today, particularly by Christians. People who advocate for social justice don't normally have the shoot-out at the OK Corral in mind. Instead, they are advocating for a decent quality of life for those who are marginalized, for the inclusion of the excluded, and for the redressing of past wrongs. These are good and worthy causes. In the justice equation, they focus on those who have been wronged and so have not received their due. But the cause is still rooted in the logic and rhetoric of justice, that each person has something due to them and if they do not receive it then the situation needs to be set aright. It is a logic that, several steps down the line, can lead to rage and anger.

It is noteworthy that Jesus himself almost never used the word justice. It was barely in his vocabulary. Justice does appear in many English translations of the Old Testament. There's the famous prophetic passage often quoted by Martin Luther King, Jr., for instance: "Let justice roll down like waters and righteousness like an ever-flowing stream" (Amos 5:24). But in these instances justice is a translation of the Hebrew word *mishpat*, which can also be rendered as judgment. In other words, it is God's judgment that needs to roll down like waters. Because God is God, God's judgment is synonymous with justice, which leads to the translations in many of our Bibles. But judgment for God looks quite a lot different from giving to each what is their due. It looks like a God who heard the cry of enslaved people in Egypt and rescued them "not because you were more numerous than any other people" but because God loved them (Deut. 7:7). It looks like a God who sees God's people profaning God's name in exile and decides not to abandon them, as they have abandoned God, but comes to them and says, "A new heart I will give you, and a new spirit I will put within you; and I will remove from your body the heart of stone and give you a heart of flesh" (Ezek. 36:26). Most of all, it looks like a God who takes human flesh and comes to dwell among God's people—and once incarnate to do things like remind his listeners about how God's love extends to all people whether they deserve it or not.

There is a mouthful of a Greek word that is used at several key moments in the gospels: *splanchnizomai*. It literally means to be moved in one's guts or bowels. In the ancient world, that part of the body was seen to be the seat of emotion, much as the heart is today. More colloquially, therefore, *splanchnizomai* is often translated as something like compassion. When Jesus is approached by a widow seeking help, he "has compassion" on her and raises her son (Luke 7:13). When he sees the hungry crowds, he is moved to feed them by that same compassion (Matt. 14:14). When the Samaritan traveler sees the wounded man by the side of the road, he too is "moved with pity" and goes to help (Luke 10:33). When the father of the prodigal son sees his son trudging along the road back home, he is "filled with compassion" and runs out to embrace him (Luke 15:20). Each of these instances are translations of the same word, a word used only in reference to God, Jesus, or their parabolic stand-ins. Each refers to the same deep physical reaction—being moved in the guts—to the suffering and pain of others. It is what marks Jesus' ministry. It is an essential description of God's very nature.

In my mind, compassion is closely linked to another word: mercy. It is merciful when Jesus tells a story about farm laborers who receive far more than they are owed at the end of a long work day (Matt. 20:1–16). It is merciful when Jesus takes his message of abundance and feeds the hungry multitude, and not just the Jewish multitudes but the Gentile ones as well. It is merciful when the messiah who has been crucified after a sham trial in a kangaroo court comes back preaching not vengeance but peace. Mercy is not about giving people their due but disregarding any considerations of what is owed and offering abundance in its place. It is this mercy that Jesus teaches and demonstrates in his ministry. It is this mercy that is at the root of the forgiveness he offers. It is this mercy that is the precondition for the reconciliation he effects on the cross. This is Christian gospel, good news. In his life, death, and resurrection, Jesus foreswears the vengeance he omitted in his inaugural address and offers us a path to new life. It is a path that leads not to rage and vengeance but one that leads to peace, compassion, and mercy.

Yet it is this mercy that is absent in a society consumed by vengeance and rage. These may make us feel good—for a time—but they do not offer a solid foundation for building human society. By contrast, a focus on mercy offers a much firmer foundation. Mercy prompts us to look at each other with compassion and ask what it is that other people are struggling with, not how they are obstacles to realizing what we want. Focusing on mercy also makes us look inward at ourselves and recognize our own mistakes, our frailty and sinfulness, and our tendencies toward rage. Sometimes, the most important person we can receive mercy from is ourselves.

The gospel of Jesus Christ is good news because it provides the only firm foundation for a sustaining and sustainable way of living. It makes us look inward at ourselves and recognize our mistaken visions and our tendencies toward vengeance and rage and says to us, "I don't think this is going to lead to the kind of life you really want." Blowing up at an airline attendant, store clerk, or bank agent is not going to address the crises of our time. When we are enraged, when we want to throw people off of cliffs, Jesus walks through our midst and says, "I left vengeance out of my ministry. Now let me show you another way." That other way is the way of mercy that Jesus preached, lived, and enacted. It is only that mercy that will guide us through this rage-filled, crisis-shaped world.

THESIS EIGHT

Christian witness is rooted in hope—even if we don't want it to be

In the first spring of the COVID-19 pandemic, there was a profusion of rainbows in Montreal. During those first weeks of social distancing and stay-at-home orders, the apartment windows in my neighborhood were covered in hand-drawn artistic creations. Many were accompanied by the same French slogan: "ça va bien aller," which can be translated as, "It's going to be fine." Pretty soon I started seeing these words everywhere—on the side of ambulances, on bumper stickers, and on the suddenly ubiquitous bottles of hand sanitizer in the grocery store.

Perhaps it is only principals of theological colleges who think in these terms but I was struck that these rainbows were making a profound theological statement. They were speaking in eschatological terms. Eschatology refers to the "last things"—*eschaton* is the Greek word for last or end—and it more broadly refers to the future and particularly to God's action in the future. In Christian terms, eschatology places Christians on a timeline of God's action, looking back to what God has done in the past, looking around to what God is doing in the present, and looking forward to what God will do in the future. These rainbows were making important claims about the future: things might be tough now, but everything is going to be alright in the end.

Perhaps one of the hardest parts of living in a crisis-shaped world is the sense of foreboding that can come with thinking about the future. People leave their homelands and search for new places to live because they are searching for a better future for themselves and for their families, but this future and its realization are fragile and uncertain. Climate change, it is clear, will continue to unleash havoc in weather patterns for decades to come. Indeed, a new word—solastalgia—has been coined to describe this distress caused by environmental change. Rather than nostalgia, which refers to the melancholy people feel when separated from a beloved place or home, solastalgia refers to the distress people feel from environmental change that takes place while they are in their homes. It is the feeling of being homeless in one's own home, of having lost the certainty and dependability that once felt so familiar.[1] If this is what the present is like, we can reasonably think the future is nothing to look forward to. Meanwhile, across many parts of the world, birth rates are in decline. This is a trend with many causes but at least one part of it is people deciding not to have children because of their fear about what the future might hold. Of course, all of this is if we think about the future at all. The force of our economic structures, as we have seen, encourages us to focus on the present moment, to consume, to purchase, to acquire the next new item now with little regard for where it has come from, how long it will be part of our life, or how quickly it will need to be replaced. In a crisis-shaped world, the very fact of the future is either deeply uncertain or deliberately ignored.

That is part of what made those rainbows so noteworthy to me. They were relentless in their focus on the future. It was clear why they were doing so. By offering assurance about the future, they provided hope now. And in that early stage of the pandemic, I was in desperate need of that hope. As was the case for many other people, the pandemic forced on my family and me a difficult change of lifestyle. I was not used to spending so much time at home, to educating and entertaining my children throughout the day, to communicating with so many people through a computer screen. What made those initial weeks and months of pandemic shutdown feel so different is that they were a kind of eschatological time. That early period of the pandemic brought the relationship between how we live now and how we can live in the future clearly into view. Public health restrictions such as wearing masks, maintaining social distancing, and keeping schools closed were about the present. They were hard: they made the present moment painful and difficult. To live in this fashion, I had to give up many common habits and patterns of relationship—no matter how appealing they were—because I learned that they would not curtail the spread of the virus. But the reason we gave up our common habits and patterns of life is that there was a promise of a future reward. These restrictions would curtail the spread of the virus and reduce its devastation. We had to live in the present in anticipation of the future. This is the very definition of eschatological living. And the fundamental eschatological virtue is precisely what those rainbows were trying to encourage: hope.

It is one thing to articulate, as I have been trying to do, an alternate ethos to ground Christian witness in a crisis-shaped world. But attentiveness, enoughness, catholicity, and mercy can seem like impossible goals in the face of the grinding reality of daily living. It is easy to despair, to abandon hope, to let the powers of this world run roughshod. That is why underlying all Christian living in a crisis-shaped world must be the countervailing power of hope. When we believe God will act in the future, we can live confidently and hopefully now. It is this hope, formed from living now in anticipation of God's future action, that is the great virtue Christians have to model for the world. To do so, we will need to reclaim our eschatological inheritance.

* * *

Scripture and the Christian tradition are packed full of eschatological material. It is there when the prophet Isaiah channels God's voice to offer a message of restoration and renewal to a people in exile: "I am about to create new heavens and a new earth; the former things shall not be remembered or come to mind. . . for I am about to create Jerusalem as a joy, and its people as a delight" (Isa. 65:17, 18). It is there on Christmas when we celebrate the first coming of the Prince of Peace while also, in the words of "It Came Upon a Midnight Clear," looking forward to the days "by prophets seen of old, / when with the ever-circling years / shall come the time foretold / When peace shall over all the earth / its ancient splendors fling, / and the whole world send back the song / which now the angels sing."[2] God will act in the future, the hymn tells us, and the song of peace that the angels sing to the shepherds in announcing Christ's birth will be sung back to heaven by all the world. Eschatological thinking is there in an affirmation made in the congregation's response in many Eucharistic prayers: "Christ has died. Christ is risen. Christ will come again." It is there, perhaps most fundamentally, in the prayer Jesus taught his followers: your kingdom come, your will be done.

In each of these examples, there is a relationship created between the present and the future. God will act to create a new heaven and a new earth, and this can be a message of hope and reassurance to Isaiah's readers. We pray for God's kingdom to come or listen for the song of angels even as we live in the midst of a broken and fallen world. If a neoliberal economy is intent on keeping us focused on the present moment, eschatology takes account of our present while keeping us relentlessly oriented toward the future. This is why hope is so characteristically associated with eschatology. If you believe that God has acted to give God's people fullness of life in the past and you believe God will act in the future to fulfill all things, then you can be hopeful. In the catechism of the Episcopal Church, in reply to the question, "What is the Christian hope?" we are taught, "The Christian hope is to live with confidence in newness and fullness of life, and to await the coming of Christ in glory, and the completion of God's purpose for the world."[3] Hope is to live now in expectation of what is coming in the future—and to know that what is coming is undeniably and overwhelming good.

Eschatology is a basic tenet of Christian theology and Christian living. However, in many mainline Protestant churches in recent generations, eschatology has been relatively muted. Future-oriented Christian thinking has, in the popular imagination, been colonized by certain interpretations of eschatology that speak of the Rapture, Tribulation, and various other loosely Biblical ideas. The used-book shelves that are heaving with the *Left Behind* series of novels are testimony to the popularity of this approach. They are also a reminder that eschatological thinking can often, though not always, go hand in hand with apocalyptic thinking. On this view, God's future action is closely related to God's defeat of the powers that are unveiled in apocalyptic visions.

At the same time, hope has become somewhat debased. "I hope so" is said in response to a wide range of questions, often quite insignificant: is it going to be sunny tomorrow? Hope is easily confused with optimism, an overly naïve view that the future will be bright, happy, and prosperous. Yet from another perspective, it is hope itself that can seem naïve. Indeed, I have heard the new word "hopium" used—a neologism formed from hope and opium—to refer to an irrational optimism that acts like a narcotic in how we view the world. It is too easy to look at the world—both now and in times past—and be overwhelmed by the scale of challenges facing us. Instead of hope, we give into despair or, its close cousin, cynicism. Optimism and cynicism seem quite different from each other but what they share is that each fails to engage the world as it really is. Each leads us to draw closer into ourselves and care less about the world around us. God's future action comes to seem remote or implausible. It is this context that makes reclaiming hope such a vital task. But if hope is not optimism and if it needs to be defended against cynics, what is it and how can we find it?

* * *

The 2006 movie *Children of Men* is based on a 1992 P.D. James novel of the same name. The main character, Theo Faron, lives in England in the not-too-distant future. The human race has lost the ability to reproduce. Women cannot get pregnant and there have not been any births in years. There is a present, but there is no future. Without a future, people begin to lose hope. Playgrounds and schools are closing down. Everyone knows they are the last people living on earth. The last generation of children to be born are now teenagers and they live with a nihilistic joy, wrecking what they encounter and disregarding everyone else. Older people are encouraged, and sometimes forced, to kill themselves at the behest of an authoritarian English government that has taken over following general apathy in democracy. When Faron meets one of the members of the ruling council, he is told, "Whatever man has done for good or ill has been done in the knowledge that he has been formed by history, that his life-span is brief, uncertain, insubstantial, but that there will be a future for the nation, for the race, for the tribe. That hope has finally gone except in the minds of fools and fanatics."[4] In other words: no future, no hope. At the same time, global instability has led to widespread migration. The authoritarian government imports so-called "Sojourners" from poorer countries to have them do the work no one else will. These Sojourners are all deported at age sixty when they are no longer useful. In the movie version, many migrants—called "fugees," a shortened version of refugees—are warehoused in distant camps, forcibly held in appalling conditions.

In the midst of all this, Theo Faron lives in an isolated, individual world of his own creation in a depopulating Oxford. He takes consolation in his books, music, food, wine, and nature. He insists in his diary, "I don't want anyone to look at me, not for protection, not for happiness, not for love, not for anything." His beliefs are simple: "That once I was not and that now I am. That one day I shall no longer be."[5] He understands that there is a past, present, and future but it is an entirely individualized timeline. He has no sense of being part of any broader timeline of human society, let alone God's action. However quietly, he too is giving into despair. Through a chance series of events, Theo meets a young woman who is, miraculously, pregnant. Suddenly, there is a future. Here the plot of the movie diverges from that of the book. In the movie, Theo ends up working with a group of people to escort the young woman to a fabled ship that will apparently be passing by the British coast and will be able to help her with her birth and protect her baby. The trouble is that to get there, he and the young woman need to go directly through one of the most notorious refugee camps at precisely the moment when a group of refugees are rising up in insurrection and the government is launching a heavy-handed military response.

There is no optimism in *Children of Men*. It is impossible to feel that way when seeing the condition of a nihilistic society that is oppressing its own citizens and abusing immigrants. Neither the movie nor the book, it is clear, will have a "happy" ending. But once Theo joins the cause of helping this woman, neither is there despair nor cynicism. Everyone understands the task they are undertaking is immensely difficult and probably impossible. They fight and disagree with each other about the best way to help and their ultimate purpose. But it does not cause anyone to suggest they might as well give up. Everyone involved is fully committed to the work because they can clearly envision what the future will be: the first birth in a generation. It is this certain knowledge of the future—pregnancy leads to the promise of birth—that provides the rock-solid ground for the hope that motivates all the characters. Hope arrives precisely because it shows everyone that a future—however fragile-seeming it may be—is possible. One by one the group of people Theo was working with to accompany this young woman fall away, through death or abandonment. People who help them along the way are killed. By the end of the movie, Theo and the young woman are traversing a dangerous zone of urban warfare. They have no one else and nothing else with them, except each other and the promise provided by the pregnancy. Without spoiling the end, suffice to say that this is, just barely, enough. Hope is not a gauzy sense of optimism or a warm feeling of positivity. Hope is a gritty, hanging-on-by-your-fingernails, no-options-left kind of virtue.

Cynicism and despair are much easier than hope. They allow us to seem confident and look popular in an apparently clear-eyed take on how awful the world really is. But despair is not the path that Theo chooses, and it is not the path Christians are to choose either. At one point in the novel, when Theo is approached about joining the group around the pregnant woman, he is told, "The world is changed not by the self-regarding but by men and women prepared to make fools of themselves."[6] The directness of this moves Theo away from his self-regarding despair in the comforts of Oxford and converts him into someone who seems like a fool to others, risking everything for the fragile hope of a future. It puts me in mind of Paul's words to the Christian community in Corinth: "For the message about the cross is foolishness to those who are perishing, but to us who are being saved it is the power of God" (1 Cor. 1:18). Despair might seem right to those around us but it denies that God is acting and will continue to act as God has done in the past.

* * *

The early weeks and months of the pandemic were a relatively brief window when the connection between the way we live in the present and the future that way of living would lead to was clear. But absent a global pandemic, eschatological living is much harder. *Children of Men*, with its vanishing future, was prescient. To again return to the reports of young people reporting not wanting to have children, giving birth may be the most future-oriented action humans engage in. Again, there are many reasons people do not have children but one of them is surely a hopelessness and concern about the future. When I see the deterioration of democratic government in some western nations and the enthusiasm for authoritarianism among some voters, I wonder if this too is not a symptom of a failure to believe in a future. Democratic apathy and a too-easy embrace of facile solutions are among the results. In a much different register, meanwhile, many Christians are asking serious questions about the future of their churches, including predicting its demise within a generation. In each case, the specifics of the problem may be different from *Children of Men*, but the situation of lacking a clear future is similar. Little wonder then that there is a widespread mood of despair and cynicism abroad, both in society and in the church.

Hopeful living is not only about looking toward the future. Eschatological living also allows us to cast a critical eye on the way we live now. If we know how God will act to fulfill all things, we are called to live now like we believe the future will one day be. It is the future disclosed in the apocalyptic visions we considered in a previous thesis, a future of new creation, right relationship, and the overthrow of oppressive regimes. It is the future written about in eschatological passages in Scripture and the hymns we sing, of joy, delight, and peace. The pandemic and a crisis-shaped world more generally revealed and reveal the deep imperfections of our social structures. When we think and live eschatologically, we are able to bring these questions of judgment to the fore and act boldly in our communities. All of this is rooted in an eschatological orientation for our living: directed toward the future, believing in God's fulfilling action, and seeking to live now like we believe the future will one day be.

The Episcopal Church's catechism tells us that Christian hope is about living "with confidence in newness and fullness of life." I love that word confidence. It literally means "with faith" but its modern usage has moved away from this. Still, there is something valuable here. No one wants to be cocky or overconfident but there is nothing quite like the feeling of watching someone do something confidently—or indeed doing something confidently oneself. I remember once visiting a glass-blowing factory and marveling at how confidently and smoothly the craftsmen moved around their workshop, heating the raw material in the furnace, turning it and shaping it, and producing delicate, beautiful creations. I could only imagine how nervous and uncertain I would have been in that environment, afraid of the hot ovens or of breaking something. But these craftsmen had the confidence that comes from the well-grounded faith in their own skills developed over years of experience. What had come before was the basis of their faith for the new creation that was emerging. This is the confidence with which Christians are called to live: with faith in what God has done and knowledge of what God will do, we can look to the future expectantly.

What that looks like is not unlike what it looked like for Theo Faron. Theo's journey toward hope in *Children of Men* began by recognizing that there was a future. He then engaged himself in the messy reality of the world. Rather than walling himself off in a comfortable prison of self-regard, he moved away from this isolation and into deeper relationships of mutuality with other people. What Theo did is also a description of the ministry of Jesus. Jesus was part of God's action in the world and pointed to a transforming future. Jesus' incarnation represented God's deep engagement in the brokenness of the world. Jesus' ministry was marked by working toward deeper relationship with all those around him. For Jesus, and in his own way for Theo, the result was a transforming hope.

I am not optimistic about the direction of either human society or the Christian church in a crisis-shaped world. The crises we encounter are simply too deeply rooted to be transformed overnight. The forces arrayed against God's people are significant. The Christian faith will continue to be pressed to the side, marginalized and de-centered. But neither do I despair about the future of our world or the church. I know that God has acted to sustain God's creation and God's church these many centuries and will continue to do so now. Ringing in my ears are the clear eschatological words of Jesus that the gates of hell will not prevail against his church. I cannot say at this time what that will look like. Nor can I predict how the future of human society will unfold. But my eschatological belief is the ground and source of a deep and abiding hope in the future of Christian witness in a broken world. Hope is not what I would choose if I had to. It does not make me comfortable or put me at ease. But it provides the confidence necessary for all resistant and countervailing living and action against the powers of this world. Christians can live and act now in hope and with confidence because we know God is acting and will continue to act in the future. Truly, in God's economy, ça va bien aller.

RESISTANT PRACTICE

THESIS NINE

Place matters: Christian witness begins in particular and specific locales

In seminary, I spent a semester abroad at Westcott House, a theological college of the Church of England. In my first week there, I sat down to dinner next to one of my new fellow students. She was approaching graduation and already knew where her first church job would be. "How big is your parish?" I asked. What I meant by the question was how many people came to church on Sunday. Her reply nearly made me fall out of my chair: "About 15,000 people." Without missing a beat, she moved into a description of the socio-economic character of the community where she would be working, its demographics and cultural diversity, the educational background of its residents, the number and type of schools, and the kinds of business and work opportunities that were present. At the time, my North American mind essentially understood parish and congregation as interchangeable terms. In the Church of England they manifestly are not. Parish referred to a particular place, a geographically bounded territory. For this student, it was this territory that would shape her ministry, not simply the people who worshipped in the parish church on Sunday morning.

This understanding of parish ministry is hardly a new concept. Indeed, in the Church of England it is a very, very old one. When I later lived in England, I worshipped in a parish that was mentioned in the Domesday Book, the census that William the Conqueror ordered after his victory at the Battle of Hastings in 1066. On the church wall hung a board that listed the rectors of the parish dating in an unbroken stretch to the early eleventh century. The rootedness in place that parish ministry describes has long characterized the Church of England's understanding of its ministry. The phrase "parish ministry" puts local, particular places at the heart of Christian life and witness. The fact that I, who had grown up in the United States and Canada, found all this so surprising was an indication of how vestigial parishes have become in the tradition in which I was raised. For many Christians in North America, parish has little meaning. Yet in a crisis-shaped world, Christians need to recognize anew the importance of place in shaping our witness.

* * *

The significance of place became clear to me, as it did for many others, during the COVID-19 pandemic. By its very nature, the pandemic was a global event, a function of an interconnected global world. At the peak of the first wave of the virus, when so many people around the world were in some form of lockdown and restricted movement, I found myself paying obsessive attention to news from around the world: access to ventilators in New York City, the health of the British prime minister, or the formation of a "travel bubble" in Canada's Maritime provinces.

At the same time, I was discovering my local neighborhood in new ways. I didn't have much choice. At the time, Montreal's leaders were strongly encouraging us to, if possible, stay within the borough of the city in which we lived. I live in a part of Montreal just outside the downtown core, full of residential housing. Many of the streets have alleys behind them. Like many others, to get out of the house and stay sane, I would go on walks around my neighborhood and explore these different alleys. Each one was different and I began to delight in noticing these differences—here a little lending library box;

there some fresh herbs planted for community use—and thinking of ideas I could take back to my own little patch of alley. Meanwhile, my family found an outlet on a nearby bike path. When the first lockdown began in mid-March, there was still snow and the bushes growing alongside the path were deep in their winter hibernation. As the weeks passed, however, we marveled as the bike path came to life and spring sprung: snow melted, bushes blossomed, and birds started chirping. I distinctly recall the bike ride we took in early May when I caught a big mouthful of bugs and realized that new life had returned. Though I had lived in the neighborhood for several years, it took a global pandemic for me to actually discover the place where I lived.

This was true more broadly as well. Although I initially paid attention to the news about the progress of the pandemic around the world, what I was really concerned about, I realized, was my particular place. Were schools open in Montreal? If not, when would they be? What was the growth rate of the virus in Montreal and how was that affecting decisions about business closures and social distancing rules? The questions that were most pressing to me were the ones about my local community. The pandemic revealed an important truth: the world we live in is one that is simultaneously shaped by global flows, such as the movement of a virus, but also one in which the actual lives of so many people are shaped by very local existence, perhaps as local as the neighborhood or back alley in which one lives.

This should not be a surprise to Christians. The Bible, particularly the Old Testament, offers a number of stories about the significance of particular places to the religious experience of God's people. Abraham, Isaac, and Jacob, and their families seemed to spend a lot of their time building altars to remember God's action in particular locations. When Jacob woke up from a dream in which he saw angels ascending and descending, he said, "Surely the Lord is in this place—and I did not know it!" (Gen. 28:16) He then anointed the rock he had been sleeping on to mark the holiness of the location. Later, the religion of God's people shifted to a more exclusive emphasis on Jerusalem as the dwelling place of God and the center of the Jewish faith. When Jerusalem was conquered by the Babylonians and the people deported, it was not just the military conquest that led to lamentation and a deep sense of loss, but their forced removal from a place of such religious significance. God's people related to one another and to God by locating themselves in particular places. The vision of God's future action that early Christians held before them was a place-based one as well. Jesus told his followers he was going to "prepare a place" for them (John 14:2). The final vision in Revelation is of a new place, the new Jerusalem descended from heaven where God dwells with God's people. Revelation describes that new place in exquisite detail, an indication of the way in which it is the culmination of God's action in the world. None of this should come as a surprise. The pressures of globalization may forestall this recognition but strong communities are still formed because of a place that people share in common.

Perhaps the strongest place-based sentiment in the Christian faith is also one of its most quoted: Jesus' command to love one's neighbor as oneself. The neighbor is literally the one who is near to us, the one with whom we share a place. In a global world, we are, if not physically nearer, at least relationally nearer to more people than ever before. But it is important not to lose sight of the literal meaning of this word. Christians are called to love those with whom they share a location. The nature of the place where we find ourselves shapes our ministry. Loving our neighbor might look different in an urban setting than it does in a suburban or rural one. That means that to love our neighbor we need to have a clear idea of the place we inhabit. Churches in the Anglican tradition have long emphasized the importance of "common prayer." But if we understand that ministry begins in knowing our place, then we should also be thinking about the ways in which our ministries serve as "common ground" for people to meet one another and work together. A neighborhood is not just a place where we live. It also describes a way of living in that place, in which we seek to relate to and know those neighbors who share that same place.[1]

Emphasizing place is important for another reason as well. As we saw in a previous thesis, there is much in the modern world that presses toward the global and away from the local. These pressures come, in large measure, from the nature of our economic structures and the influences of a market-based economy. In its zeal for growth, market economies push away from local particularity and toward homogenization. The more that consumers are the same, the easier it is for the market to serve the greatest number of them. Place is a necessary antidote to this. Each place—each neighborhood, each alley—is distinct and unique. Rather than obliterating this, we should nurture these places and, through them, form local, communal identities.

It was my time in England that first started me thinking about place. But there was always one aspect of Christian witness there that I found puzzling: the fondness for equating England with a new Jerusalem. It is a view most clearly expressed in the popular hymn, "Jerusalem," based on a William Blake poem of the same name. The first stanza asks a series of questions such as "And did those feet"—meaning Jesus'—"in ancient time / Walk upon England's mountains green?" The answer to this question, and all the others in this verse, is a firm no. But the hymn concludes with the suggestion that "the green and pleasant land" of England can be a place where the English people can build Jerusalem. I have been part of many a congregation that has sung this hymn with great gusto—and I certainly appreciate robust congregational singing—but I find in it a warning about place. It is possible in forming attachments to particular places that we become so convinced of their specialness and importance that they need to be defended from all external forces. This can become a form of idolatry: the place can come to displace the God who created it and whom we meet in that place. The Christian call is to hold our attachments to place both deliberately but also lightly, to allow those places to be permeable and open. Christian places are places that are attentive both to those within the place and those seeking to join. The neighbors we love are not an unchanging cast of characters. Rather than seeing our places as Jerusalem, we can see them as a stop on the way to the new Jerusalem which we will never fully attain in this life but which is the end of all our witness. In the next thesis, I'll say more about Christian witness at a time of global migration. Suffice to say now that in a world shaped by the ongoing movement of people, the permeability of Christian places is especially vital. This permeability offers a welcome to newcomers and invites them into existing place-based communities that are, by that welcome, continually reshaped, reformed, and renewed.

* * *

Shortly before the pandemic, I took some of my students to Waswanipi, a community of Cree people several hundred kilometers north of Montreal, not far from James Bay, the body of water just south of Hudson Bay. On that visit, we spent time with Allan Saganash, a Cree man deeply steeped in his people's culture. Allan had spent much of his life on the land as a hunter and trapper. He showed us maps of his trapline and could identify the place where he had been born in a tent alongside a lake seventy years earlier, the places where his children were born, and good locations to find beaver or moose or good wood for making shelter. He talked about how the Cree understand the year to be divided into six, rather than four, seasons, with each season determined by what can be done on the land. He talked to us about the place of beavers in their landscape, how they can be hunted for their fur and meat but also how they play an important ecological role in creating habitats for other creatures. Beavers are important not just in the income they generate or food they produce but for their place within the entire ecosystem.

Allan had recently retired from a forty-year career as a land manager for his local tribal government. In the 1970s, the Cree people of James Bay had signed a land claims agreement with the government of Quebec in which they received different kinds of rights over different parcels of land. It had been Allan's job over the intervening decades to negotiate which pieces of land fell into which category and to fend off timber and other resource development when it happened in the wrong places. He told us about the never-ending series of meetings he attended, the maps he produced, and the detailed, painstaking work to protect trap lines, spawning grounds, camp sites, burial areas, and so many of the other places that are central to Cree culture. It sounded exhausting. One of my students asked him what kept him going. "I guess you could say it's because I'm Cree," he said. "This is our land. This is how we live." It was a message we heard from other people in the community as well. When we heard stories from members of the community who had survived many years as students in church-run residential schools that sought to deprive them of their culture and language, many told us how the only way they reclaimed their culture was by returning to the land. One survivor told me how when he returned to his Cree community after a seven-year absence, he immediately went to "the bush" for two years. "It was the land that gave me my culture back and reminded me who I am," he said. When we discussed all this afterward, one of my students marveled, "When Allan speaks, it's almost like the land is a character in his life. You can hear it said with a capital letter."

When my colleague at Westcott House told me about her parish, she focused exclusively on the people who lived there and what her ministry would be like in response to their life in that place. Increasingly, however, it is becoming clear that it is not just human life in a place that matters but all life—human, plant, animal, fungal, bacterial, and so much more. This is, in part, what is referenced when Indigenous people refer to the land. For many Indigenous peoples, the land, including the waters around it and all life on it, is constitutive of identity and central to culture, life, and livelihood. There is much to learn from Indigenous peoples' relationship with the land and the best way to do this is through spending time with Indigenous people on that very land. But in this thesis, I want to highlight one aspect that seems especially important in a crisis-shaped world.

As Allan Saganash's experience demonstrates, by dividing and categorizing the land, land claims agreements have tended to commodify it. This ensures that Indigenous peoples need to relate to land through nonindigenous and specifically colonial categories. The land becomes a site of natural resource production—around Waswanipi that is primarily timber—rather than a place in which, say, the gift of the beaver can be received. Indeed, the reason Allan had those maps handy to show us is that the community had to produce them to demonstrate the significance of their use of the land to government officials charged with economic development. One way in which Indigenous approaches counter the commodification of the land is by understanding the land as a gift. It is a view clearly expressed by the Indigenous author and scientist Robin Wall Kimmerer in her book *Braiding Sweetgrass*. She offers what might be called the parable of the wild strawberries to demonstrate how the land is understood as a gift. As a child she picked wild strawberries every year for her father's birthday. The presence of these strawberries taught her that land—understood here to mean the whole natural world and the life it supports—is a gift that came to her through no action of her own: "you cannot earn it, or call it to you, or even deserve it. And yet it appears. . . . Gifts exist in a realm of humility and mystery."[2] Understanding these strawberries as a gift, she practiced self-restraint and tried not to take too much but just enough to make a pie for her father's birthday. Kimmerer contrasts the gift economy with her experience of a capitalist economy of private property, in which self-restraint is not a virtue. The accumulation of more is. On such a view, private property is necessary to the accumulation of profit and the consequent rejection of the land as a gift. Kimmerer asks how we can come to understand the land and the earth as a gift again and "make our relations with the world sacred again?"[3] Kimmerer's story is a demonstration of a deeper truth. When our ethic is rooted in the land it means that the people—who are, after all, only one part of the life on the land—do not set the terms for life on the land: the land itself does. This knowledge of limits, so foreign to a world shaped by an ethos of more, is a piece of wisdom that comes from rooting ministry in the land. It is wisdom that is deeply needed in a crisis-shaped world.

* * *

The church in a crisis-shaped world is called to be a church that is rooted in both place and land. It is a church that will be attuned to and sensitive to the needs and concerns of the local community. But it will also be attentive to the nonhuman life in that place as well. Many churches are already taking steps in this direction. The movement toward gardens and farms on church-owned property is an important way of relating both to place and land. Another model, called "watershed discipleship," calls on Christians to be intentional about living their Christian discipleship in their particular watershed.[4] I appreciate these ministry innovations. But we can also recognize that place and land are already present in our liturgy, with latent potential to shape our witness.

The offertory is the moment when bread, wine, and money are brought forward and offered to God on the altar. In the Anglican tradition, the words often associated with this come from

1 Chronicles 29: "All things come of thee, O Lord, and of thine own have we given thee." The sentence is part of a prayer King David offers when he is about to die and hand over everything to his son Solomon. David prays:

> But who am I, and what is my people, that we should be able to make this freewill offering? For all things come from you, and of your own have we given you. For we are aliens and transients before you, as were all our ancestors; our days on the earth are like a shadow, and there is no hope. O Lord our God, all this abundance that we have provided for building you a house for your holy name comes from your hand and is all your own (1 Chron. 29:14–15).

Both the familiar, abbreviated version and the longer passage highlight several significant points related to land and place. As humans we are dependent on God's creation, and but one part of a larger community of creation that God has created and set us in the midst of. We are also impermanent dwellers in this place. David describes himself and his predecessors as "aliens and transients," language that is akin to a later tradition, as we shall see in the next thesis, of referring to Christians as exiles. Even as he calls himself an alien, David announces his desire to hallow a particular place by building a temple as a dwelling for the Lord. David recognizes that alienness and rootedness are not contradictory. It is possible to be of a place but also originate in another place entirely.

More broadly, the offertory is a reminder of what we can call God's gift economy and its rootedness in the first gift of Creation. There is a historic offertory prayer adapted from a Jewish prayer that makes this explicit: "Blessed are you, Lord God of all creation: through your goodness we have this bread to set before you, which earth has given and human hands have made. It will become for us the bread of life."[5]

God gives all of Creation, not because of anything we have done but out of the abundance of God's love. From this gift, the congregation receives what is necessary—bread and wine—to give thanks—the literal meaning of Eucharist—to God. The offertory is a reminder of our dependence on others, on God's creation, and above all on God. In celebrating the Eucharist, we are also acknowledging and being reminded of the web of human and nonhuman relationships of which we are a part, which are rooted in a particular place and part of creation, and which find their origin in God.

If we are serious about what the offertory means, then Christians are called to be people who take seriously where we are. The bread and wine (and the flour and grapes behind them) come from some place specific on the land. It is time to start asking where. More broadly, we can ask questions about ourselves as well. We are embodied and in a specific place as well. Where are we? What is this place? How is this land related to our lives? Who has been on this land before us? Who is newly arrived on this land with us now? Many of us are so out of touch with our land and places that it may be difficult to answer these questions at first. But as my colleague at Westcott House recognized, ministry is not simply about those in church on Sunday but about all in that place and, we can add, all life on that land. In deepening these connections, we can find a literal grounding for our witness in a crisis-shaped world.

THESIS TEN

In a time of widespread migration, Christians must embrace their identity as wanderers as well

On a trip I made to Nigeria once, I spent two weeks staying with an Anglican bishop and his wife. At dinner on the first night, they served fish in a nut sauce with fried plantains. It was delicious. I complimented the bishop's wife, telling her how much I appreciated the food, especially the plantains. She must have spread the word because as I traveled around the diocese and was the guest of other priests and their wives, there were the exact same fried plantains at every meal. I understood the impulse. They wanted to welcome me as their guest and make sure that everything was just right. If that meant swapping stories among each other, well, that was just what they had to do to ensure they showed hospitality. As a guest, however, the hospitality became a bit oppressive. By the last night of my visit I had just about had enough plantains to last me for a lifetime. Yet as a guest I was in no position to say, "I am sick to death of these and cannot possibly eat another bite!" Instead, I complimented my hosts, effusively, and swallowed yet another—delicious—plantain.

The guest–host relationship has long been central to human relations. Indeed, it was probably more central to the ancient cultures that shaped the world of the Bible than it is to our own. The word that is used to describe the relationship created when a host welcomes a guest is hospitality. The Bible offers many examples of this relationship, as well as its absence. Abraham welcomed three strangers under the oak trees at Mamre who turned out to be angels

(Gen. 18:1-8). The cities of Sodom and Gomorrah were destroyed because, the Bible tells us, they had "excess of food and prosperous ease but did not aid the poor and needy" who migrated into their midst (Ezek. 16:49). In other words, they were insufficiently hospitable to those who needed it most. This emphasis on hospitality makes sense in a world in which survival was in question, journeys were dangerous, and it was often only the kindness of a stranger that was the difference between making it to the next day and not. This kind of hospitality was characteristic of the ancient world precisely because those offering hospitality knew that one day they could be in need of food and shelter.

The relationship of hospitality is a complex one and has varied across time and cultures. But in many contexts, particularly in western society, it is a relationship shaped by a basic inequity. As my experience with plantains reminds me, it is the host who determines the contours of the hospitality. While my hosts in Nigeria were often able to ensure that their hosting was not the central feature of their participation, they nonetheless set the menu, prepared the food, showed me where to sleep, and arranged for me to meet other people. The host chooses to offer their resources to welcome a guest. Likewise, while I offered small gifts to my hosts, as a guest I was primarily the one who was receiving—in this case, plantains! This inequity is not bad. I could have opted out of it by paying to stay in a hotel and arranging my own meals. But this would have impoverished my experience of the country and the church. It would have robbed both my hosts of the delight they took in offering me warm hospitality and the delight I took in receiving it and thinking of ways I could one day reciprocate.

It is an obvious statement but worth making: in order for the guest-host relationship to be formed, the guest has to move. This may be as simple as taking the subway over to a friend's house for dinner or as involved as flying to Nigeria. But at least until the invention of video meetings and the lockdowns of the pandemic, human movement was necessary to enact hospitality. This is especially important to remember in a crisis-shaped world. One of the great facts of the early years of the twenty-first century has been human migration. More than ever before, people are on the move. This migration takes many forms. Bankers, lawyers, consultants, and other professionals work for multinational firms in countries outside their country of birth. Students move to seek education abroad. Temporary workers travel to a new country for income that they send home to support family members. The pandemic put a temporary pause on some forms of human movement, but it came rushing back as restrictions were lifted. In many western countries, the share of the population that was born in another country is at the highest level in a century or more. I know what this is like. Although I now live in the country of my birth, I have lived, worked, and studied in two other countries of which I am not a citizen, and traveled to many others. This movement has been part of the privilege of my background.

Human migration also includes the category of people who have less choice in their movement. This includes people who are forced to flee their homes in the face of violence and war. It also includes people who leave climate-stressed parts of the world or places where they feel they have little future to look for new opportunity elsewhere. Border areas of the world—such as the U.S.–Mexico border, Roxham Road in Quebec, or the Mediterranean Sea—have at various points in recent years, received intense media attention that crystallizes, though not always helpfully, the reality of this movement. These border areas have also become increasingly dangerous and deadly to the people seeking to cross them.

The movement of people is not new to human experience and on its own it does not constitute a crisis. But several aspects of the current situation are different from what has come before. The first is the sheer scale of movement. Given the diversity of forms of movement, firm numbers are difficult to come by but in 2022, the United Nations High Commissioner on Refugees reported there were over 110 million forcibly displaced and stateless people in the world, up from less than 70 million in 2017. This group includes internally displaced people, who flee their home but not their country of nationality and so are not formally classed as refugees; refugees who have fled their country of origin and are unwilling or unable to return and are afforded specific protections under international law; and asylum seekers, who are seeking international protection but are not yet sure what assistance they will receive.[1] A second novel aspect is that countries lack clear agreement about how to respond to this movement. International agreements that were meant to govern the response to refugees and asylum seekers were crafted after the Second World War, a period much different from our own. These agreements seem less and less relevant as the nature and relative ease of migration changes, media coverage of migration blurs important distinctions, and some political leaders wield immigration as a cudgel against their opponents. Different countries have different visa regimes, different requirements for entry, and different pathways to legal residency. The issues can quickly become maddeningly complex. People who are citizens of the country in which they live can conveniently ignore these complexities, while those who are not citizens must pay them constant attention. With continued instability and growing wealth gaps between rich and poor parts of the world, people will continue to be on the move. The ongoing intensification of the climate crisis will further complicate migration and challenge traditional understandings of why people move and what protections they deserve. How to encounter people on the move will remain a crucial question for global society in the coming decades.

The language is not always used explicitly but there is often an implicit expectation that migrants will, at least initially, have a relationship of guest to the hosts in the country where they arrive. In Canada, for instance, the private refugee sponsorship program has allowed faith communities to join together to raise funds, arrange housing, and help find work for people from overseas. The faith community takes on the role of host to the guest family that is arriving. By contrast, some of the rhetoric that raises questions about migration argues that migrants will take resources that are rightly spent first on citizens in the receiving country. In other words, migrants will become guests in an environment in which it is argued that guests cannot be afforded. Widespread human migration will repeatedly confront all of us with the question of hospitality and the nature of the guest-host relationship. At a time of strained resources and fraught global relationships, the inequities in the guest-host relationship, themselves a reflection of inequities in our global world, are coming under more pressure. To minister in this migratory world, Christians will need a robust understanding of what our faith has to say about hospitality.

* * *

The Bible is packed full of advice about how to respond to migrants, and that advice is straightforward: welcome them! The story of Abraham welcoming the strangers at Mamre is a parabolic version of teachings that appear elsewhere in Scripture. The law code in Leviticus commands the Israelites that "The alien who resides with you shall be to you as the citizen among you; you shall love the alien as yourself, for you were aliens in the land of Egypt" (Lev. 19:34). The language is parallel to the commandment to love one's neighbor as one's self, a commandment that Jesus will make central to his teachings and which first appears just fifteen verses earlier in Leviticus. God's people knew what it was like to be strangers and wanderers. Abraham and his sons had moved around the Holy Land and the Israelites had wandered through the wilderness for a generation on their way out of slavery in Egypt. When it came time to summarize who they were, they began with words that identified this migratory heritage: "A wandering Aramean was my ancestor; he went down into Egypt and lived there as an alien" (Deut. 26:5). Because they had been migrants, they were called to love strangers in the same way they were called to love those who were already near them. In an earlier thesis, I pointed to a verse from the First Letter of John: "we love because he first loved us" (4:19). I now offer another substitution: use "welcome" for "love" and say "we welcome because God first welcomed us." In the same way that God's grace welcomes us into God's forgiving embrace, we too are called to welcome others. Another way of saying this is that we become hosts because God first hosted us.

However, there are at least two problems with thinking of migration solely in terms of welcome. First, in relation to white mainline Christians in North America, no manner of gracious hosting can obscure the fact that Christians inherit a legacy of being bad guests to the original inhabitants of these lands. Second, thinking solely in terms of welcome does not disrupt the inequitable relationship inherent in the guest-host relationship. When Christians like me whose ancestors have lived in a land for several generations and achieved a measure of economic comfort see themselves as hosts to migrants, it can lead to powerful and important ministries of hospitality. But it does not guard against an all-too-human tendency that most dinner party hosts have felt at some point in their life. It is the tendency to say, "Why won't they just go home? I'm done being a host." This is one description of the response that many people are having as they look at the growing numbers of people on the move in the world.

Jesus complicates and challenges received wisdom on hospitality. The gospels have many stories of him attending meals as a guest. But occasionally, as in the case of Zacchaeus the tax collector, he was a rather odd sort of guest. When Jesus shouted at Zacchaeus up in a tree, he was essentially inviting himself over for dinner (Luke 19:1–10). Outside of the Last Supper, there are rarely stories of Jesus serving as a host in anything like a classic understanding of that word. But that did not stop him from violating any understanding of good manners and teaching others how to be better hosts. Once, while eating a meal at the house of a Pharisee, Jesus decided the time had come to offer some advice on how to be both a good guest and a good host. He told the guests not to sit in the place of honor but to sit in the lowest place. He offered some unsolicited advice on how to create a guest list: "When you give a luncheon or a dinner, do not invite your friends or your brothers or your relatives or your rich neighbours, in case they may invite you in return, and you would be repaid. But when you give a banquet, invite the poor, the crippled, the lame, and the blind" (Luke 14:12–13). To be a host in the way of Jesus is to invite not those people who can give to you in return but those who are most marginal and from whom you have no hope of ever being invited in return.

More fundamentally, Jesus' Incarnation is a moment of becoming a guest. God's transcendent Word comes to dwell with humans, but does so as a helpless baby in a manger, who needs the support from a mother and father who welcome him as their own and become his hosts. One way of phrasing the truth of the Incarnation is that God in Christ allows himself to be welcomed by humans, that is, to become the guest of humans. To return to the passage from First John, not only can we substitute welcome for love, we can go further and say, "We allow ourselves to be welcomed because God in Christ first allowed himself to be welcomed." In other words, we become guests because, in the Incarnation and then in his ministry, the Son of God first became a guest.

It is not surprising, therefore, that the Bible never lets its readers forget two things. First, God's people are to be welcoming to strangers. This, as we have seen, was fundamental to the logic of the ancient world. But second, and more unusually, God's people are also to remember that they too are migrants. It was true in the Old

Testament when God's people remembered themselves as descendants of a "wandering Aramean." It is true in the New Testament as well. In the First Letter of Peter, for instance, the readers are addressed as "exiles"—a particularly challenging kind of movement—and enjoined to "live in reverent fear during the time of your exile" (1:1, 1:17). As followers of Christ, the messiah who was on the move virtually from the moment of his birth, Christians are reminded that we too are always migrants—guests—in this world. We are, to use a phrase sometimes evoked, a "pilgrim people" on our way to another destination that is not of this world. Scripture seems quite clear that extending sympathy and welcome to migrants and interacting with people on the move are necessary steps to following in the way of Jesus. But they are only first steps. The Christian tradition also leaves us with a more challenging question: in this situation of hospitality, how can I be not simply the host but also the guest?

* * *

Christians are among the many people who have moved around the world in recent generations. When these migratory Christians arrive in new locations, they often seek to form a Christian community, known in the scholarly parlance as diaspora churches. When I first arrived in Montreal, I spent a Sunday morning visiting a local congregation of the Redeemed Christian Church of God. The RCCG is a Pentecostal mega-church founded in Nigeria that has a stated vision of having a church "within five minutes walking distance in every city and town of developing countries and within five minutes driving distance in every city and town of developed countries."[2] At the time of my visit, that congregation was one of five they had in Montreal. The one I visited met in a rented room above a mechanic's shop. Some diaspora churches worship in more traditional church locations, although they do not often own them. In Montreal, it is not uncommon to see a church sign that advertises a mainline Protestant church—Epiphany Anglican Church, for instance—and then, right next to it, another sign advertising something like the Montreal Korean Community Church meeting in the same building a bit later in the day.

By necessity, these diaspora churches have learned how to be guests. They often need to rent space, whether from a car mechanic or another church. More significantly, these churches grow in large measure through continued migration. The RCCG's growth strategy is at least implicitly premised on the continued movement of Nigerians around the world. In diaspora congregations, it is not uncommon to find people who specialize in immigration law and can help orient newcomers to the country and assist them as they navigate the process of securing a new legal status. There is a constant interplay between being a guest in a new land while also being a host to those who come after. By contrast, the mainline churches who host these congregations fall naturally into the role of host. When conflict between the existing congregation and the diaspora congregation happens, and it does, there is little doubt about who is in charge.

The presence of these diaspora churches reminds Christians in the North Atlantic world of several important facts. First, as if we needed another reminder, people are on the move. Second, part of our Christian identity is to not just welcome others but to allow ourselves to be welcomed, that is to be guests. In a crisis-shaped world in which human migration is an increasing and inescapable fact of life, it might be worth trying on the role of guest from time to time. If another church worships in your building, have you ever been to that service? If another church opens in your neighborhood, have you ever reached out and gotten to know them? It may not be possible to form a relationship with a church from a diaspora of which you are not a part. But given the sheer scale of human movement in this world, it is almost certainly possible for someone who has been long settled in a place to form a relationship with someone who has recently arrived. That relationship cannot simply be one of host and guest. The person who has been long settled must seek ways to actively become the guest of, to receive from, the one who has recently arrived.

The fragility of the church at this point in its history has led some congregations to shed property as they age and shrink. Seen within the context of the guest-host relationship, this shedding of property may actually be beneficial. Losing one's building does not need to mean losing one's identity as a congregation. But giving up the building will almost certainly make it difficult to think of oneself as the host all the time. Indeed, it may even force people who are used to being hosts to become guests for a while. I think of an Anglican congregation in Montreal that sold its building to another Christian community and then agreed to rent back the space for ninety minutes on Sunday morning. The Anglican congregation moved its service forward to 9 a.m. and agreed to be out of the sanctuary by 10:30 so the new community could start their service at 11. They negotiated the use of the hall for special occasions and ensured their priest still had an office in the building. But the Anglican congregation, which had owned the building for decades, now found itself a guest in its former home. While this may have been unusual at first, it has transformed the ministry of the congregation. Rather than having to focus their energy and effort on maintaining the building, they are now freed to connect in a deeper fashion with their community, including with the new congregation that owns their building.

There is a tension between this thesis and the previous one when I argued that Christian witness needs to be rooted in place and land. In this thesis I have been arguing that Christians need to understand themselves as migrants and exiles who receive welcome. If we are to be on the move, how can we be rooted in place? If we are rooted in place, how can we understand ourselves as migrants? This tension is not new and, indeed, it is encapsulated in language to which I have already pointed. When the author of First Peter addresses his readers as exiles, the Greek word is *paroikos*, which literally means the one who is beside or outside the house. The one who is outside the house is the wanderer, the one who is in need of hospitality. It is a surprise, therefore, that the English language has taken this Greek root and turned it into the word "parish." (The connection is seen most clearly in the English word "parochial," the adjectival form of "parish.") But parish ministry, as I suggested in the previous thesis, is often used to describe rootedness in place, not foreignness.

In a world that is unceasingly shaped by global flows of ideas, goods, and above all people, it is vital that Christians remain aware of this global world and be rooted in particular places. But that rootedness in place is not contradictory with the idea that they are also meant to be guests in that place. "Parish ministry," therefore, is not the staid preoccupation of out-of-date vicars. Rather, it expresses the central tension of the Christian identity: rooted in place but also an alien wandering in a strange land. These were not contradictory ideas for Jesus the guest-host. Nor should they be contradictory ideas for us. In a global world, Christians are rooted in place, open to new wanderers, ready to be guests to those they encounter, and open to where the Spirit leads us on our wandering journey of faith.

THESIS ELEVEN

Public, shared places resist the dominance of the market. Building them up is part of Christian ministry

In the center of Cambridge, England, there is a fancy shopping center called the Grand Arcade. It is not unlike any of the high-end malls that have emerged in upscale parts of the world, offering themselves as destinations for consumption and a day out. The Grand Arcade also implicitly offers itself as a kind of public square. It is situated along a well-traveled path from one side of town to another and it has easy access to foot traffic. Even with no intention of shopping, it is a place one might find oneself often passing through. After all, it looks and feels a lot like a shared space for a community.

Looks are deceiving, however. One day when I had about half an hour to spare between meetings—not long enough to make it to the university library to kill time but too long to go to my next meeting early—I sat down in the Grand Arcade, pulled out my laptop, and started doing a little work. It didn't seem strange to me. There were people in a café not twenty feet away doing the same thing. After a few minutes, I became aware of someone standing next to me. I looked up to find a security guard looking at me. "What are you doing, sir?" he asked, in a not unkind but direct voice. I explained how I was killing time. "I'm afraid you can't do that, sir," he told me. "I'll need to ask you to move somewhere else." The Grand Arcade was not, in fact, a public space. If I wasn't willing to participate in the consumption around which the Grand Arcade was organized by at least entering a café then I wasn't permitted there. I found the security guard's request annoying but the hardship was bearable. It was theoretically possible for me to get a tea at the café and wait out my time there. Instead, I left the Grand Arcade and walked—slowly—to my next engagement. For people without my privileges, such as those who are precariously housed or without adequate financial resources, then the Grand Arcade's faux public nature would be much more of a challenge. It is a challenge that is only becoming more commonplace. The increasing dominance of the market and market-oriented values is displacing public, shared spaces. It is a challenge not only for those on the margins of society but also for Christian witness.

* * *

For much of recent history in western society, it has, in the broadest terms, been possible to describe two domains or spheres of activity in which humans live their lives. On the one hand, there is a private domain. In the language of the ancient Greeks, who thought about this division a lot, this was the *oikos* or household. It included members of what is today called the nuclear family. It also included other people who were part of the household, including slaves as well as more distant family members who shared the home. The decisions in this sphere are the decisions about how to structure one's family or how to generate income. More broadly, it is where decisions are made about such weighty matters as who to marry (when people have been free to make those decisions), how to educate children, what religion to practice, and how to lead one's life.

On the other hand, there is a public sphere. Again in the language of the ancient Greeks this was the *polis*, the root of the English word political. The public sphere contains within it many different domains. It is here where decisions regarding the common good are taken, such as how to distribute the resources a society generates, how to govern a society, whether to make war on a neighbor or seek peace. It is in the public sphere that members of the community come up against those from different backgrounds and learn how to live together in equitable fashion. The public sphere is easily recognizable in national or provincial legislatures. It is equally present at the very local level as well. During the pandemic, some of my neighbors petitioned the government of our borough to restrict car access to our shared alley to make it safer for children to play. The borough government responded by conducting a vote of all residents whose homes abutted the alley. The decision—to restrict some entrances to the alley but not all—was not precisely what my neighbors wanted. It was also unpopular among those neighbors who didn't want any restrictions at all. But it was an example of the way in which we make decisions in the public sphere about how we share our lives together in a common place. As this example indicates, the public sphere is related to places. These can be local—my back alley, for instance, or the local park and playground where I meet all sorts of people from around the neighborhood—or they can be much broader. Questions about how societies should care for the elderly, the sick, or new mothers or when and how to deploy military resources are decisions that implicate people across a vast range of places. On the surface, the Grand Arcade presents as being part of this public sphere, a space shared by all who pass through.

Historically, there's been another sphere or domain of activity. While it could go by various names, I'll call it the market. It is the place where goods are sold and traded. In English, we call this economic activity. The word economic originates in the word *oikos*. It is an indication of how the market was initially conceived as the place where households managed their affairs with certain defined kinds of activity. In this way, we can understand the market—historically at least—as a kind of subset of the public sphere, restricted to certain functions. I have already likened our market-based society to a form of religion. The language of spheres offers a complementary perspective on the market's dominance. As we have moved from having a market economy to being a market-based society, the market has come to take over territory previously in the public or private spheres. My experience in the Grand Arcade was one very small example: what presented as a public place was actually a market-based space. If I was unwilling to participate in the market activities it presented to me, then I was not welcome to remain.

Spheres may seem like an esoteric matter. But the displacement of the public by the market has had significant impacts in many parts of our shared lives. Minimum wage laws are one example. For many generations politicians have debated the wisdom of a minimum wage and the level at which it should be set. This was naturally seen as a decision located firmly within the public sphere. Locating the decision in the public sphere did not, of course, produce universal agreement about policy but it did clearly identify the forum in which the debate should be had. When labor unions or business owners wanted to seek change, they knew how to do so. But the rise of a ride-sharing company like Uber, for instance, and its many competitors, has changed the equation. Uber argues that what it is doing is simple and straightforward. It is not providing rides to people. Instead, in its language, "Our rideshare marketplace connects riders looking for transportation with drivers looking for work at the tap of a button."[1] In its own understanding, Uber creates a market that brings together drivers who have a service to sell and riders who wish to purchase that service to get from point A to point B. The price of that ride is set by the supply of drivers and the demand for rides. It is the market at work. Who can argue with this?

The trouble is that study after study has demonstrated that Uber drivers are generally not earning anything like minimum wage in the jurisdictions where they work. In Chicago, for instance, a 2022 study found that Uber and Lyft drivers earn about $13 per hour after expenses in a city where the minimum wage is over $15 per hour. In Toronto, a 2023 study found a wage range between $6 and $10 per hour when the minimum wage is over $16 per hour.[2] Uber claims that drivers are not employees but just users of the platform it has created to sell their services. As such, Uber is not obligated to pay them minimum wage. It is the market that decides how much their time is worth. What has happened, though, is that the creation of a market has displaced a decision made in the public sphere through democratic debate.

Uber, of course, is far from alone. It is only one of many gig economy companies in which people are paid by the number of tasks they can perform—gigs—rather than the number of hours they work. Food delivery companies, some package delivery companies, and freelance working apps, are other examples. Perhaps there are benefits to a society like this. Certainly, corporations like paying by how much work is done, not how much time is spent on the job. Paying by the task imposes a kind of discipline on workers and is presumably thought to improve performance, though at a significant cost to employees' mental and physical health. But it also undercuts decisions that societies may have publicly made about the nature of work, not simply regarding minimum wage but also regarding workplace safety, workers' compensation, breaks, vacation time, sick days, and a whole host of other issues. The market sphere is displacing the public sphere.

This was made clear to me one day when I received package deliveries from two different delivery men. The first driver worked for an international corporation. He drove a truck plastered with its logos, walked deliberately from his truck to my front door, greeted me pleasantly, and waited patiently while I figured out how to sign the electronic device he handed me to confirm delivery. When I looked out the window a few minutes later, I realized he was still on the street, sitting in the driver's seat and eating a sandwich. Later that afternoon, a second driver pulled up. He was driving what was obviously a private car that looked barely road-worthy. It was crammed full of packages. He grabbed mine, sprinted to my door, insistently rang the doorbell, and quickly became exasperated while I figured out how to sign for the package. With a harried look on his face, he ran back to his car and took off down the street. Curious about the differences, I looked up the two companies that were responsible for these deliveries. The first driver's company likely paid him an hourly wage, and he was almost certainly part of a union. The second driver was almost certainly paid per package delivered. He was, however hard it may have been to believe, a willing driver, and the company was buying his services one package at a time. The result in the work lives of the two drivers I saw was clear. I knew I'd rather live in a society in which more people were able to work like the first driver.

The gig economy is far from the only culprit. In a market-based society, markets are being created that displace decisions made in the public sphere. Short-term housing rental companies like Airbnb or Vrbo are creating new markets between people who have properties to offer and those who wish to rent them. The benefits of this are obvious to anyone who has traveled recently, including me. One result, however, is that the creation of these markets is raising the cost and reducing the availability of long-term housing, pushing hotel-like accommodation into areas of communities that had previously not had it, and in some cases having catastrophic consequences for safety. For instance, hotels are governed by fire regulations. In early 2023, the city of Montreal tragically discovered that some Airbnb hosts were not adhering to these rules when a fire destroyed a building that was dominated by Airbnb rentals and killed six people. The creation of a market not only displaced decisions made in the public sphere but actively worked against those decisions and goals. As more and more parts of society come to be governed by the disciplines of the market, debate over values—such as the level of a minimum wage or fire codes—disappears and is replaced by reference to price—the price of an Uber ride or an Airbnb stay. As long as there is a willing buyer and a willing seller, then there is no need for any further conversation.

The growth of the market sphere has not been by accident. It has been aided and encouraged by economists who have put forth ideas about the importance of markets and their extension to more realms of life. It has equally been encouraged by a vein of political rhetoric that has repeatedly attacked the legitimacy of many of the institutions that once dominated the public sphere, including government agencies, labor unions, and, indeed, legislative bodies themselves. The trouble is that not all—or even most—challenges can be solved by the creation of markets. We cannot address global migration or global warming without effective, coordinated action among many government and nongovernmental actors in a global public sphere. However, if public institutions are being weakened and delegitimized, they can hardly be expected to respond effectively. The ineffectiveness of this response becomes part of the case against it, furthering the delegitimization of the public sphere in a downward spiral. The unique struggle in a market-based society is that the sphere where shared debate and shared action can take place is disappearing, thus weakening our collective ability to respond to our crisis-shaped world.

A depressing summary of this transition came in a moment that took place in a 2016 American presidential debate between Donald Trump and Hillary Clinton. Clinton criticized Trump for apparently not paying any federal income tax. Trump quickly cut in: "That makes me smart," he said with a triumphant smirk on his face.[3] The existence of taxes and the rate at which they are set are among the most significant decisions made in the public sphere. For Trump to effectively claim that dodging taxes makes him smart reveals not only a lack of belief in common and effective government action or a willingness to respect decisions made in the public sphere, but also the way in which market-based values have triumphed over all others. What matters is not a culture of shared living and shared decision-making but a narrow calculation of individual self-interest, particularly as defined by income and wealth. It is a reminder that when the market is in charge, there is a natural tendency toward individualization and the forsaking of shared, common concerns. For Trump to think that this was a winning political strategy is an indication of the depth of both the market's triumph and the displacement of the public sphere.

* * *

Historically, many strands of the Christian tradition, and religion more generally, have at varying times and with varying emphases, had something to say about both the public and private spheres. In liberal democratic societies of the twentieth century, Christians have made claims about how those societies should be structured or about which policies are appropriate or desirable to pursue. The Second World War-era Archbishop of Canterbury, William Temple, laid the groundwork for the post-war welfare state in Great Britain through his writing and theology. Universal health care in Canada is largely the result of Christian preachers on the Prairies who understood the powerful need for this program and convinced society it was worth adopting. Christians have also made claims that are more oriented to the private sphere and the lives of individuals. These are views about how family life can and should be structured, for instance, or about how people should dress, behave, or otherwise conduct themselves. It is not necessary to endorse all these ideas to recognize the way the Christian tradition has seen its witness directed to both private and public spheres.

More fundamentally, churches have engaged in society's spheres through the very kind of places they create through their existence. I found myself thinking of this as I waited out the fifteen minutes after my fourth COVID-19 vaccination jab. As I sat in the basement hall of a local church, it occurred to me that all my shots had taken place in churches or, more accurately, church basements. This was somewhat surprising: the government of Quebec is aggressively secular and opposed to most forms of organized and public religion. Yet here it was making citizens of all backgrounds traipse through churches to get their shots. And it was easy enough to see why: churches occupy a peculiar kind of location. They are not private residences to which access is deliberately and reasonably restricted. Neither are they businesses, in which access is theoretically granted to all on the assumption that those who enter will contribute to the business's purpose of making a profit. Nor are they government-run places like a community center or a post office, which are open to all but are either for specific purposes (mailing a letter, applying for a passport) or are so limited and under such pressure that they are effectively only open to those with the wherewithal to book far enough in advance.

A church is like none of these places. It is, instead, similar to how the American poet Robert Frost once described home: "the place where, when you have to go there / they have to take you in."[4] Although this is not always true in reality, it does describe one vision of what churches are meant to be: when you don't know what else to do with all the stuff (for lack of a better word) you've got inside, a church can be a place to collapse into. So perhaps it was not surprising that when the pandemic dumped a whole lot of stuff onto our societies, it was natural to turn to churches as a way to deal with it, in this case through opening a huge number of vaccination clinics. It's the place we turn to when we don't know what else to do. I have already argued that Christian witness is to be centered on place. Christian communities are to be linked to the land where they are located and be a common ground for the people on that land. This thesis now adds an important qualifier to that earlier description:

Christian places are public places. They are not private or profit-seeking, but open, receptive, and welcoming.

The rise of the market sphere at the expense of the public has resulted in a society that feels somehow hollowed out. More and more of our interactions with one another are conditioned through a market of some kind. As our values are reduced primarily to considerations of price, it is easy to retreat into our private lives and see other people as, at best, instruments for our own survival. There is a diminution of a sense of shared, common life. But this diminution can be devastating to the ministry of a church. The corollary of a place-based ministry is that Christian ministry depends on a strong public, community ethos. Christian communities in part create this ethos but they also benefit from it. And it is not just Christians. The Quebec government opened vaccination centers in synagogues, mosques, and temples as well as church basements. Other faith communities are also part of the public sphere and can be allies in defending and promoting it. It does not compromise uniquely Christian witness to assert that many different faith communities have a shared interest in a robust public sphere.

What all this means for Christian witness is that part of the role of Christian communities is to identify shared, public spaces—particularly those that exist with as little reference to the market as possible—and support them. Given the place-based nature of Christian witness, this will be done oftentimes at the most local level. A church I was once part of on the South Side of Chicago identified the striking disparity among neighborhoods of the city in their access to public pools during the summer. There were far more such pools in white neighborhoods than on the predominantly Black South Side. For the congregation, this was a matter of justice. But the congregation also implicitly recognized that providing public, shared space would enrich the lives of all in the community. The congregation's members were involved in spearheading a successful campaign to open a new pool in the church's mostly Black neighborhood. Churches that understand how they can use their places to facilitate shared experiences among different members of a community are also engaged in building up the public sphere. This takes the shape of hosting debates among candidates for local office, for instance, planting gardens on its land, hosting a voting location, providing respite space for striking workers, or any of a host of other similar activities that assert that we are more than beings who exist to live private, individual lives and interact only within the confines of a market. Some of these actions depend on having a building or a place. Others, like advocating for more swimming pools, come simply from a commitment to a particular place. To be sure, a strong public sphere by itself does not on its own produce a just society. But it provides a venue in which that work can take place.

Given the global nature of the crises affecting our world, action on this scale can feel tremendously insignificant. But such action is vital because it sends a broader message that the market on its own cannot address our crises. Indeed, the market tends to militate against precisely the common, shared, and collective action that is necessary to address these crises. Christian communities, along with other faith communities, are ideally placed to affirm the importance of the public sphere in which we need to make decisions about our common future. It is in this affirmation that we will begin to find a way forward.

THESIS TWELVE

Food is at the center of the church and must be at the center of Christian witness

Food is at the center of the Christian faith. On the night before he died, Jesus shared a meal with his closest friends. His command to them to take bread and wine and "do this in remembrance of me" has led to countless throngs of Christians in the millennia since to do exactly that—to eat and drink, and in so doing, form themselves as a community before God, be incorporated into the death and resurrection of Christ, and give thanks for God's salvific action in the world. The shape of this practice has varied widely, as have the beliefs that have accompanied these actions. But the actions of eating and drinking remain central, even if in some Christian communities this link has become attenuated. As one line has it, "It's one thing to believe that the bread is actually the body of Christ. But it's quite another thing to believe those stale wafers are actually bread!" Even so, what is variously called the Eucharist, mass, communion, or a variety of other names serves as a reminder that to survive in this world, both as people and as Christians, we need to receive—food and drink for our bodies and the body and blood of Christ for our souls. In the Eucharist, we are connected to God, connected to one another, and connected to God's creation through which we receive the gifts we need to celebrate the Eucharist. Eating matters. Food matters.

The trouble is that food systems have become part of the crisis-shaped world. It begins in the ignorance that many of us have about where our food comes from. For the first time in human history, vast swathes of humanity know very little about where the food before them originated. Or if we do know, it likely comes from locations far distant from where we eat it. My grocery store in Montreal advertises blueberries from Chile and strawberries from California. The edamame I buy comes from China. The avocados come from Mexico. Neoliberal capitalism has turned food into yet one more commodity in a global world. Food products have become standardized so that they can be more easily traded. When Russia invaded Ukraine in 2022, many people far from the conflict, particularly those living in the poorest parts of the world, quickly learned how central Ukraine was to global grain and oil production. Food prices spiked, causing hunger for many people. As a commodity, the production of food mirrors that of other commodity items and tends toward homogeneity. Producers seek to maximize production, minimize costs, and ensure regular and reliable production. The result is what is accurately described as factory farming because many farms now seem very similar to factories. They rely on inputs like fossil fuel-based fertilizers or animal feed. They use advanced technology like state-of-the-art tractors and combines or animal slaughtering equipment. They produce consistent, identical products, like chicken wings that can be deep-fried in the exact same amount of time at every fryolator in the land.

The homogenization of food production might make sense if it worked. But it is increasingly clear that it does not. Unlike a factory for, say, iPhones or blue jeans, food production—the work of farming and animal husbandry—is directly connected with the natural world, and the natural world is variable and diverse. It is an ecosystem governed by its own logic and that logic is not the market-driven logic of homogeneity. When factory farming meets the natural world, the results are disastrous—initially for the natural world, but in time for those who need food, which is to say all of us.

Much of the natural fertility of farmland, for instance, is contained in its topsoil. But modern agricultural practices result in the erosion or destruction of topsoil. Topsoil is a naturally renewing product but the timeline for this is so long—decades, if not centuries—that it is effectively a nonrenewable resource. The fertility that is lost through topsoil is artificially replaced by fossil fuel-based fertilizers. Fossil fuels are an equally nonrenewable resource, of course, and one that contributes to the intensifying climate crisis. Meanwhile, much of the meat consumed in the world today is produced in so-called concentrated animal feeding operations in which animals are packed into impossibly small areas, grown for their meat, and then often inhumanely killed. Much of this meat is prepared by migrant workers, who also make up the bulk of workers on many farms. These migrants who labor to produce our food do so in dangerous conditions and constitute one of the most oppressed parts of the working class. The result is perverse. Humans produce more calories than ever before. But we are doing so in a fashion that is jeopardizing the ability of future generations to do the same, inflicting harm on creation, and exploiting people on the move. In our food system, the various strands of our polycrisis crystallize and become visible.

Meanwhile, many people do not receive enough food or food of sufficient quality and nutrition. In the same way that climate change has introduced new ideas into our lexicon, a crisis-shaped food system has as well. We now speak of "food deserts" to refer to those parts of the country that lack regular and reliable access to fresh and nutritious food. Such deserts are concentrated in poor and marginalized communities where major grocery chains find it unprofitable to operate and the only food available is unhealthy and expensive. The phrase "diseases of civilization" refers to nutrition-related complexes like diabetes, obesity or heart disease that tend to rise in countries as they adopt a western lifestyle of fast food and increased meat and sugar consumption. Whereas hunger or starvation was once a hallmark of poverty, poverty is now marked not necessarily by a lack of access to calories but by a lack of access to good and nutritious food. Obesity is as much a product of poverty as it is a product of wealth. All of this takes place while food wastage remains shockingly high. The very stuff of life is casually tossed aside as unfit for the standardizing demands of an industrial food system.

The farmer and author Wendell Berry has written that "eating is an agricultural act."[1] It is on one level a strikingly obvious statement. But it needs to be said because so many people and so much of our food system feel disconnected from agriculture. Instead of eating being an agricultural act, the modern food system has made eating into the act of a consumer. In this, it is little different from the pressures toward homogenization and consumption that are present elsewhere in our economic structures. As consumers, we are encouraged to eat food that is, to the greatest extent possible, identical. A McDonald's hamburger or a Chipotle burrito is meant to be the same wherever one happens to consume them. Moreover, like other consumer products, we are encouraged to think about food only in the moment of our eating it. Don't think about the food's past—where it came from and how it was grown—or the food's future—the long-term implications of how the food was grown. This is the natural result of a system in which the market-based values of a global economic system are allowed to extend into ever more domains of life, including the most life-sustaining of all, eating. The food system is shaped by and contributes to the crises of this world and is itself in crisis. If that crisis is not yet entirely evident or if we think we can ignore it, its reliance on the exploitation of nonrenewable resources and damaging impacts on the natural world mean it cannot be pushed aside forever.

* * *

If food is central to the Christian faith and the food system is the place where the interwoven crises of our world crystallize, then we should expect that food and eating will be places of important resistance to the powers of this world. It is natural to begin with an examination of Jesus' eating practices, which extend well beyond the Last Supper. He spent a fair amount of time eating at other people's houses. Occasionally, he saved the day like when he turned water into wine and rescued the hosts from the embarrassment of running out. At other times, he was, as I noted in an earlier thesis, a somewhat obnoxious house guest who offered pointed and unsolicited advice about how to throw a party—whom to invite, where to seat people, and so on. Occasionally, and seemingly without planning, he fed other people—lots of them, and all at once. Each gospel relates this in a slightly different fashion, but it seems Jesus was remembered to have fed large crowds of people at least twice, in one case more than five thousand and in another over four thousand. In these stories, Jesus points to a different relationship with food, one that moves outside the boundaries of the market, away from consumption, and toward a posture of gift and reception.

As the Gospel of Mark (6:30–44) tells the story, Jesus withdrew to a deserted place with his apostles for a rest. But the crowds that had been hanging on his every word followed him. Rather than resting, he taught them. As the day drew on and it became late, his apostles had this piece of advice for Jesus: "send them away so that they may go into the surrounding country and villages and buy something for themselves to eat." The advice is laughable. They are in a deserted place. The closest food is a long way away. Moreover, there are thousands of people, likely far more than those villages could feed. What is especially striking, however, is the verb, *buy*. The apostles think that the primary way to relate to food is through purchase.

For them, food is a product of the market. In his reply, Jesus changes the verb: "You *give* them something to eat." The apostles reply: "Are we to go and buy two hundred denarii worth of bread, and give it to them to eat?" It is a huge—and expensive—amount of bread they are considering, for a huge crowd. They have heard Jesus' use of the word "give" but they cannot break out of the mentality that sees food as something to be purchased. Sure, they might be thinking, we can give people bread but someone has to buy it first.

In reply, Jesus asks them how much bread they have. When he hears it is five loaves and two fish, he gets the people to sit down in groups. Taking the bread and fish, he looks to heaven, blesses it, breaks it, and gives it to the disciples to give to the people. In other words, he acknowledges the God who has created all things and blesses the bread that comes from God's creation. Jesus probably gave the bread to his disciples to give to other people to help speed the process of distribution. But I like to think he did it so that the disciples realized they could give bread to others without having to buy it first. It was the disciples who were the first to see this miracle, the miracle that food is part of a giving and receiving relationship, not a purchase and consumption relationship.

Given the centrality of eating and feeding to Jesus' ministry, it is not surprising that he included food in the prayer he taught his followers. I learned this line in the Lord's Prayer as "Give us this day our daily bread." The verb is important: give. Not "let us buy" but give to us so we may receive from you. The word for "daily" can be translated as "what is necessary for existence" which renders the petition as "give us this day the bread that is necessary for our existence." The prayer is not asking God for bread to stuff ourselves full with but neither is it asking to be left hungry. The petition asks not for more but for enough bread. Since we are asking for bread for this day, we are called to pray this prayer every day. The prayer is an inducement to look into the future and think about future days when we will be asking God for this daily bread. When I consider the modern food system and the damage it does to the earth, I wonder what it will be like to pray these words ten, twenty, or more years from now. What will our relationship with the earth be like then? Will it be such that the earth can produce sufficient food to provide enough for all who dwell here?

* * *

In several previous theses, I have mentioned that a market-based society encourages those of us who live in it to regard ourselves as consumers. This is how the great benefits of globalization were sold: global trade flows would (and indeed did) expand the range of goods available to us and lower their price. It is why one of the most successful companies of the era of globalization—Wal-Mart—can have as its slogan "everyday low prices." But as the politics of the last generation have taught us, humans cannot simply be reduced to their needs for consumption. It is this inchoate yearning to be recognized as something more than just a consumer that has, in part, been responsible for the convulsion in western politics.

The industrial food system is likewise rooted in a mentality that prizes consumption. It provides a wide range of food products from around the world at prices that are, notwithstanding recent inflation, historically low. In keeping with the capitalist mindset it makes these goods available to those who are able to pay. The most nutritious and most diverse range of goods are available in the upscale grocery stores of suburban shopping centers. For those who can't pay, it is a food desert of limited choice and limited nutrition. It is not far from the logic that Jesus' disciples rely on: let everyone *buy* something for themselves, even when they are standing in the middle of a literal desert. If you are a consumer first, your own consumption needs are your own problem and not anyone else's.

This is obvious but the crises of our world mean it needs to be said repeatedly: the Christian faith understands people as more than consumers. People are created in the "image of God" and that God is a creating, loving, and giving God, not a consuming one. As I have already suggested, I find this vision realized in part in the vision of the Christian community offered in the pages of the New Testament. There, the Christian community is described as the body of Christ. This vision is rooted in the belief that all members of the community are given gifts. These gifts are part of who a person is and they are not meant for the person to keep to themselves. Instead, the body of Christ is meant to be an environment in which these gifts are constantly being shared with others. In other words, members of the body of Christ are people who are constantly giving to others and—equally as important—receiving from others. If people just sit back and consume, the full maturity of the body of Christ cannot be realized.

In my second year of seminary, my class went on retreat. Though it was meant to be a silent retreat, at one point one of my friends said to me, "I think we're going to get Eucharist soon." It was meant as an innocuous comment about the schedule. But there ensued an only-in-seminary kind of conversation—in whispers. I objected to my friend's verb: get. "The Eucharist isn't something you get," I said. "It's not like a new book or a new pair of shoes or whatever. You *receive* the Eucharist." It may not have been the proper place for the conversation but I stand by the point. The Eucharist is a gift from God and the only proper verb to use with a gift is receive.

But the Eucharist is also a reminder that we have something to offer as well. It's why there's a moment called the offertory when the congregation brings forward its gifts of money and bread and wine. I've already written about the offertory in a previous thesis. What I want to emphasize here is the way in which the offertory underscores the mutuality of relationship inherent in the body of Christ. In order for me to receive the Eucharist from God, I need to be in a community with someone who can make bread (or buy wafers) or someone who can contribute money to do so. I may be that person for someone else. When I stand in line or kneel at an altar rail or wait for a shared plate to be passed around a table or any of the many other ways to receive the Eucharist I am reminded that all these people with me are also called to follow Jesus in one body with me. I have something to offer them and something to receive from them. The Eucharist, therefore, is a culmination of Jesus' teaching to his closest followers when they confronted a hungry multitude. By moving beyond an economy of consumption rooted in buying food, Jesus enabled those followers to see the way in which they could receive gifts—in this case, food—from him and offer it to the hungry crowd and do so in a way that moved beyond the logic of consumption. The food practices that are at the heart of the Christian faith are a reminder that all of us are called to be both givers and receivers.

If Christians are called to resistance in a crisis-shaped world, then that resistance will necessarily challenge the reduction of human identity to that of consumption. Food practices are a vital place in which to enact this resistance. One of the things I have learned from gardening is that my garden is not like the produce aisle in my grocery store. I can't go in and pick out what I want, when I want it. Instead, I need to learn to receive from my garden the gifts of its produce. This means I don't expect tomatoes in May, for instance, but I might expect asparagus. I look for strawberries in June but I don't expect cantaloupe until July. But I am not just receiving from the garden. I also contribute to its production. I grow a far more diverse range of legumes than are available in my grocery store—orca beans and black chickpeas, obscure varieties of black beans and large runner beans that originate in Indigenous communities. Because I garden in a community garden plot, I am constantly receiving advice (and seeds and seedlings) from my neighbors while also offering some in return. The pollinating insects offer their vital services in return for the flowers I plant and the blossoms of my vegetables. Ultimately, all of this produce is a testament to God's good creation and my role in working with and within this creation to offer my gifts and receive what God has to offer me.

When I get in the kitchen, the logic is the same. I receive what God has given me and I work with it to produce food that sustains me in my service to God. I am, at best, a disinterested chef but I so admire watching others cook and work in the kitchen. I love seeing the creations that emerge from people who delight in having others over for dinner parties. The delight comes from the recognition that in that moment cooks are expressing an identity as a creator and producer and offering that to others. That is what God does in creation and it is that image in which we are made. Not everyone gardens and not everyone cooks. But each person is called to express the identity of both producer and receiver clearly and often, and to do so at least in part through our food practices.

I want to return to the story of God's people being fed with manna after they fled from Egypt (Exod. 16) that I referred to in an earlier thesis. Its place in the story is important. The first fifteen chapters of Exodus have seen them through the plagues, out of Egypt, and across the Red Sea. In chapter 15, they celebrated. Now they face the harsh reality of their trek through the wilderness. It is perhaps not surprising that they start complaining about what they are missing from Egypt. The adrenalin rush of escaping from slavery has faded, and their needs are much more prosaic. What this means is that essentially the first encounter with God that this newly freed people has concerns food. Perhaps God made this first because of the centrality of food in the Egyptian empire they are leaving behind. These same now-freed people had previously been building storage cities for Pharaoh to keep the grain in. One of their ancestors, Joseph, had administered this system for a time and done so in an economy that emphasized sale and consumption, including with his own brothers. What the people of God setting out into the wilderness need to understand is that food is the point of demarcation for them. It represents what they are leaving behind and it points to the provision God will ensure for them. If they cannot understand that, then they will never understand the way of life toward which God is leading them.[2]

As it was for God's people in the wilderness so it is for Christians in a world in polycrisis. Food is central to Christian witness in this crisis-shaped world not simply because the food system is in crisis and itself crystallizes the nature of our current polycrisis. Food is central because it is in relating to food that we are offered a vision of what Christian discipleship is about, constantly producing and receiving. It is a vision that stands in powerful contrast to the vision of a market-driven world that seeks to reduce humans to consumers focused only on the present. The Christian vision of who humans are is significantly more expansive and significantly more delightful to inhabit than the identity of a homogenous consumer. It is that identity that grounds the practice of resistant living in the world.

RENEWED CHURCH

THESIS THIRTEEN

In a mistrusting world, the church is called to be a community of responsibility and solidarity

When vaccinations against COVID-19 became available, I was eager to receive mine as soon as I became eligible. But it quickly became clear that some people did not share this eagerness. There was a contingent of people in Canada, in the United States, and elsewhere who were reluctant to get vaccinated or flatly refused. The reasons for the objections varied. There were concerns about safety. How could something that had been developed so quickly actually be safe? There was also an ornery objection to getting anything that was mandated by the government, as it was in some places. But often the objection simply boiled down to these words I heard from a neighbor: "I'm not getting vaccinated. I don't believe in it."

The use of the word believe struck me as particularly revealing. In English, *believe* can have at least two different meanings. At Christmastime when a child is asked if they believe in Santa Claus, they are being asked if they think Santa exists. At a basic level, believing in something or someone is to think it exists. For my neighbor, it was not that they did not believe vaccinations existed. The clinics were just as obviously located to her as they were to me. My neighbor had a deeper objection, related to a further meaning of believe. Belief can also mean something like trust. That was the objection of my neighbor. For whatever combination of reasons, she just did not trust the vaccine.

My neighbor, of course, was not alone. The advent of vaccinations against COVID-19 also saw the mainstreaming of a long-standing "anti-vax" movement that led to resistance to vaccine mandates and encouraged people not to get vaccinated. High-profile politicians, professional athletes, and other elite figures offered their support. In Canada, it led to a massive protest in Ottawa that paralyzed the city for weeks by drawing individuals—and trucks—from across the country to occupy the nation's capital. There were many reasons for the anti-vax movement. But a central reason for the success it had is surely what was revealed by my neighbor's comments: trust—or more accurately, a lack of it. The angst and turmoil that surrounded a mass vaccination campaign was an indication of a broader breakdown in social trust. That decline in trust is part and parcel of a crisis-shaped world.

On one level, it is hard to fault my neighbor for not trusting the guidance of elected leaders and public health officials. The movement from the seeming stability of the 1990s to the polycrisis world of the 2020s is, in part, the story of a decline in trust—often for very good reasons—in politicians, businesspeople, and other societal leaders. When China joined the World Trade Organization, people in western countries were promised that this would ultimately be a benefit to them, in lower prices and better jobs. Instead, more than a million manufacturing jobs disappeared in the United States and the communities that relied on those jobs began to feel hollowed out. That may not all have been due to China's accession to the WTO but it sure didn't help. The American-led war in Iraq that began in 2003 was justified to the public as a means to find and destroy the weapons of mass destruction Iraq was allegedly building up. No such weapons were ever found, but the cost—in human lives and dollars spent—was staggering. In 2008, the global financial system cratered, causing untold havoc for homeowners, retirees, and the huge number of young people entering the job market for the first time. The bankers who presided over the financial system were never punished but millions of other people suffered the consequences. It seemed like there were two sets of rules, one for the wealthy and well-connected and the other for everyone else. It is not just political and economic leaders. The church has been complicit in the breakdown of trust as well. The sexual abuse revealed in many churches—and emphatically not just in the Roman Catholic church—is a demonstration of how those in whom so much trust was placed failed to honor that trust and instead abused it, causing grievous and long-lasting harm. In their own way, each of these moments created conditions that led to polycrisis. With each failure, it became easier for people not to believe what those who were meant to be leaders in society were saying.

Indeed, this mistrust formed the basis for whole political campaigns. For me, the epitome of this view came in the 2016 campaign in Britain to leave the European Union. An interviewer confronted Michael Gove, one of the chief proponents of leave, with a lengthy list of academics and elites who opposed leaving the EU. Gove replied: "I think the people of this country have had enough of experts with organizations with acronyms saying that they know what is best and getting it consistently wrong." Just a moment earlier in the interview, he had linked his comments explicitly to trust: "I'm not asking the public to trust me," he said. "I'm asking them to trust themselves."[1]

"Trust yourself" is a good line if you are trying to support a friend who doubts their ability. But it is not a helpful concept to build a society on. Societies need trust in order to function. When I enter an elevator, I need to trust that it has been inspected by someone trained for the job and certified as safe. When I drive over a bridge, I need to trust that it is being regularly maintained and repaired. When I buy food, I need to trust that it has been prepared in a safe and sanitary way and won't harm me. And when the normal functioning of society goes awry, as it sometimes does, I need to believe that investigations will happen and people will be held accountable to ensure it does not happen again. Ultimately, social trust is necessary for human and societal flourishing.

The opposite of a trusting community is a suspicious and fearful one. It is a community in which people feel justified in retreating from engagement with people outside their social circles and drawing more closely in on themselves. It is a community in which it is easier to be hostile, unkind, or just simply indifferent to other people. It is a community that feels not unlike how many people experience a crisis-shaped world. It is, as I noted in a previous thesis, one that Pope Francis describes as characterized by a "globalization of indifference." If we do not trust one another, we are not likely to care for one another. It becomes easier to ignore the suffering of others, retreat into our own worlds, and trust only ourselves.

* * *

The Book of Exodus is about many things, including the freeing of God's people from slavery in Egypt, their wandering in the wilderness, and the giving of the law. But there is one question that pervades the story, appearing at the beginning and then again at the end: who is God? The narrative of Exodus really gets going when God reveals Godself to Moses in the burning bush and tells Moses to go to Egypt to free God's people. The always-inquisitive Moses has a question in reply, "If I come to the Israelites and say to them, 'The God of your ancestors has sent me to you', and they ask me, 'What is his name?' what shall I say to them?" (Exod. 3:13). In other words, who are you? In response, God says, "I am who I am." It's a bit of a head-scratcher. I am, well, what? But it's enough to get Moses on his way to Egypt, see him through his confrontation with Pharaoh, and lead God's people across the Red Sea into the wilderness and on their way to the Promised Land. The name God gives in reply to Moses also results in a name for God: Yahweh, which is a form of the Hebrew word to be. I am.

The question of who God is comes again to the fore toward the end of Exodus. Moses has been given the tablets of the law but destroyed them once he saw the people worshipping a golden calf in the place of God. But God is faithful to God's people and indicates a willingness to give the law again. As Moses is about to receive the new tablets, he again asks to learn more about who this God really is: "Show me your glory, I pray" (Exod. 33:18). In other words, show me what you are really about. God agrees and passes before Moses on the mountain. As God does, God says, "Yahweh, Yahweh"—in other words, "I am, I am"—"a God merciful and gracious, slow to anger, and abounding in steadfast love and faithfulness, keeping steadfast love for the thousandth generation" (Exod. 34:6). At last, this is the content that describes the initial "I am." There is much rich meaning in this identification and in its longer elaboration, not all of which I have quoted here. These words become central to how later generations will understand God. They appear again in the psalms, in the prophets, and in other writings as a repeated reminder of who God is.

In this thesis, I want to highlight especially the phrase: "steadfast love and faithfulness." Steadfast love is a translation of a single Hebrew word, *hesed*, a word that describes the bond of love that characterizes a covenant. It is a love that is constant, unyielding, unwavering, and, well, trustworthy. In case we did not get the point, it is paired with the word "faithfulness," which is simply another word for trustworthy. God is many things. But close to the core of God's identity is this: God is a trustworthy God. Throughout the rest of the story of God's relationship with God's people told in the Hebrew Scriptures, God stays true to this self-description. Time and again God re-forms this covenant with God's people—"you will be my people and I will be your God"—and demonstrates the rightness of this self-identification, continually being with God's people at the most challenging and difficult of moments.

For Christians, the ultimate proof of God's trustworthiness comes in the form of Jesus Christ. Christ's Incarnation demonstrates the steadfastness of God's love in a new way, by taking human flesh and sharing life with God's people. By Christ's obedience to God to the point of death on the cross, he demonstrates, in the words of Paul, that "neither death, nor life, nor angels, nor rulers, nor things present, nor things to come, nor powers, nor height, nor depth, nor anything else in all creation, will be able to separate us from the love of God in Christ Jesus our Lord" (Romans 8:38–39). Jesus himself often spoke about trust, though it is not always immediately obvious. We see it when he speaks about faith and belief. The first words of his public ministry include these words: "believe in the good news" (Mark 1:15). Throughout his ministry, he often reminded people, including his closest followers, to believe. "Do not let your hearts be troubled," he said on his final night alive. "Believe in God, believe also in me" (John 14:1). Closely related to this was the word faith. When he healed people, he told them, "Your faith has made you well; go in peace and be healed of your disease" (Mark 5:34). These words are related to each other. To have faith in something is to believe in it, and vice versa, and each points toward trust. Likewise, when Christians affirm their faith in the words of one of the historic creeds of the church, they begin with the word "believe." A creed is an expression of faith and thus begins with belief. But this belief is not just about existence but about trust. When Christians affirm that we believe in one God, we are asserting not only that the one God exists but that we place our trust in this one God whose existence we affirm. It is what

Jesus is saying to his followers when he tells them to believe in him: trust me. It is the trust that people placed in Jesus that he responded to when he healed them. The Christian faith is centered on a trustworthy God and the response to that trustworthy God is to offer our trust—our faith, our belief—in return.

What we learn from the New Testament, however, is that the relationship of trust is not simply between God and God's people. In order to follow Jesus, followers of Jesus need to trust one another as well. As we have seen in earlier theses, to live in the body of Christ is to be in a society in which people are meant to be constantly giving and receiving gifts to and from one another. This can only be done when people trust one another and try new things, take new risks, and venture in new directions. When the Acts of the Apostles describes the early Christian community as one in which "all who believed were together and had all things in common," it is worth reflecting on the faith in one another that such a community depends on. It takes a lot of trust to give up control of your possessions and believe that the community will "distribute the proceeds to all, as any had need" (Acts 2:44–45). But that is precisely what Scriptures tell us the early community did—not perfectly and not always but often enough that it became remembered as a hallmark of the community. This should not be a surprise. The Nicene Creed affirms that Christians believe in—place their trust in—the church. Given all that the church has weathered across its millennia of existence, it is easy to look skeptically at this claim. But it expresses a truth about the communities of followers God creates. A steadfast and faithful God—a trustworthy God—leads to communities founded on trust in which those followers can place their belief.

* * *

When it comes to community, trust is only the first step. An example from my childhood offers an illustration of what comes next. When I was 11 or 12, my parents began to let me come home from school by myself to an empty house. They made this decision presumably because they had trust in our neighborhood—if something really went wrong, there would be someone around to bail me out—and because they trusted me. But that trust came with something else: responsibility. I had to walk our dog and get started on my homework.

Trust and responsibility are linked, and when trust is in short supply, responsibility will also be in short supply. That is what characterizes our crisis-shaped world. It is straightforward to understand that carbon emissions today will have significant impacts on future (and indeed present) generations. But it has been difficult if not impossible to have a serious conversation about how people alive today have a responsibility to those future generations such that we moderate our emissions today. In a world marred by suspicion and mistrust, it is not surprising that some people react to the presence of immigrants from other countries not with a sense of responsibility and care but with hostility. Underlying all of this is an economic system that teaches us not to trust each other but to interact in a marketplace where, we are told, if we simply seek our own best interest the right outcome will be produced for the right price. It is hard to develop an ethos of responsibility for anyone but oneself in such an environment.

Given that many actual Christian communities have been places not of trust but of abuse and misconduct, the church cannot simply say that its response to a mistrusting world is to model trustful communities in return. It might instead be better to begin with responsibility. This could be unpopular as responsibility isn't exactly fashionable. Theologically, it is possible that if we speak about our own responsibility we are in danger of missing out on the way God's action precedes all of our own. But responsibility is never far away from what Jesus is talking about. When he tells the story of the Good Samaritan, for instance, it is hard not to see the Samaritan as the one who took responsibility for the wounded man on the side of the road. "Go and do likewise," Jesus tells his followers. More fundamentally, and as the word suggests, responsibility begins in our response to the loving action of God. God's action comes first and we respond to that love by creating trusting, responsible communities with others.

If responsibility has been muted in churches in the North Atlantic world, it has been a foundational part of the theology of some Christians from the non-western world. The Botswanan scholar Musa Dube, for instance, spent many years working with people with HIV and AIDS in her home country and reflecting on what it is like to be on the wrong end of an exploitative global economy. In reading the Lord's Prayer, she saw an "invitation to Christian communities and individuals to assume active responsibility for all that hinders the daughters and sons of God around the world to come to full realization." In looking at the damage that economic globalization had caused in her context, she saw that in praying the Lord's Prayer, Christians are called "to become responsible partners. . .in the building of healthy interpersonal and international relationships."[2]

Responsibility has also been an important part of the teachings of Pope Francis. Francis' first trip outside of Rome as pope was to the island of Lampedusa, which at the time had become a major landing site for immigrants from Africa. While there, he drew particular attention to those who had drowned while trying to cross the Mediterranean. Francis asked, "Who is responsible for the blood of these brothers and sisters of ours? Nobody! That is our answer. It isn't I; I don't have anything to do with it; it must be someone else, but it is certainly not I. . . . Today no one in our world feels responsible. We have lost a sense of responsibility for our brothers and sisters."[3] These Christians who live and have lived on the periphery of the structures of a globalized world see the centrality of trust and responsibility to Christian witness.

Once Christians begin to understand their communities as places of trust and responsibility, another step naturally follows: solidarity. Solidarity has been and continues to be used in a variety of different contexts, often well outside the church. I understand solidarity to be the act of treating the needs and concerns of another person as if they were your own, that is, to take responsibility for those concerns. (Solidarity patently does not mean telling someone what you think their needs and concerns should be and then caring about those, a besetting failure of the church across history.) In an earlier thesis I highlighted the importance of heterogeneity and catholicity in Christian community, for seeing and being in relationship with the wholeness and diversity that God calls us to. Solidarity is the cousin of catholicity. Both begin with the recognition that the church is more than simply a collection of individuals but by its very nature is a social, communal body. Catholicity calls us to whole relationships within that body. Solidarity understands those relationships to be relationships of trust and concern for one another.[4]

The challenges the church is facing in a crisis-shaped world sometimes make it difficult to imagine that the church could ever take responsibility for anything but its own survival or stand in solidarity with anyone except those who are already pledging members. This again may be the gift of the increasingly peripheral position of many churches. As churches and Christianity are pushed to the margins, Christians may find ourselves even closer to the peripheral and marginalized with whom solidarity is so important. Caring for the needs of others is a lot easier when you're much closer to them.

There is a story in the Acts of the Apostles that links trust, responsibility, and solidarity. At one point in his itinerant ministry, Paul and his companion Silas were arrested and thrown into prison (Acts 16:16–34). While sitting in their cell, Paul and Silas pray and sing, a demonstration of their trust in God. The other prisoners are fascinated by this and sit, listening to them. Suddenly an earthquake shakes the foundations of the prison. All the doors to the cells are opened and the chains are broken. When the jailer wakes up and realizes what has happened, he prepares to kill himself. He presumes, rationally, that everyone has walked free on his watch. But then he hears a voice. It is Paul shouting at him: "Do not harm yourself, for we are all here." It is a remarkable moment of both responsibility and solidarity. Paul and Silas understand themselves as responsible not simply for themselves alone. They are also responsible for the other prisoners they have just met and who have been listening to them pray and sing. What's more, Paul and Silas are responsible for the one who, just moments ago, had held the keys to their freedom. That leads to their decision to stand in solidarity with the jailer. Paul's cry from his cell indicates he recognizes what a tight spot the jailer will be in if it turns out that everyone has escaped. Paul acts on the needs of this jailer—treats those needs as equivalent to his own—by convincing everyone to stay put in prison. It is an act of responsibility and solidarity that flows from the trust that Paul and Silas have in God and in one another. The result is the expansion of the Christian community. The jailer is so stunned by what is happening that he asks what he must do to be saved. The answer? "Believe on the Lord Jesus, and you will be saved" (16:30). In other words, demonstrate that same trust in Jesus that we have and join us in this community of responsibility and solidarity.

Solidarity is largely absent in a crisis-shaped world—and it is absent in part because of an absence of trust. If political leaders are telling us to trust only ourselves (or, implicitly, them) and that no one else is trustworthy, it is difficult to care for someone else's needs. If we live in a world in which the dominant values encourage us to look out only for ourselves, it doesn't seem necessary to bother to feel responsible to anyone else. Let everyone take responsibility for themselves while the rest of us hunker down and try to ride it out. Being a Christian in a church, by contrast, means being a trustworthy person in a trustworthy community. Rather than giving in to the everyone-for-oneself mentality that leads to isolation and disconnection, Christians will naturally be people who take responsibility and stand in solidarity, particularly with those who are on the periphery. This can sound exhausting. It's just more work, isn't it, for people who are already overstretched? But that view forgets the primary action of God. To live in responsibility and solidarity is only possible because a trustworthy God stands in solidarity with each one of us and with our Christian communities in the same way that that same God stood in solidarity with an exploited and enslaved people in Egypt and walked with them through the wilderness to the Promised Land. Rebuilding trust and rebuilding community is slow and painstaking work. But a vision of solidarity stands before us and calls us toward renewed trust in God, in Christ, and through the Holy Spirit in one another.

THESIS FOURTEEN

The church's future is an ecumenical one—but a very specific kind of ecumenism

For much of my life, I have had at least a passing acquaintance with other Christian traditions. I went to a college founded by Baptists and was involved in the university chapel with a chaplain who was nominally ecumenical but did not do much to hide his Baptist background. I was also part of the evangelical campus ministry, which took me far from my roots in the Episcopal Church. Nonetheless, I kept returning to their gatherings, always convinced there was something important to learn. Later, I lived in a small town in Alaska where there was not an Episcopal Church and so found myself a member of the Methodist congregation. When I worked for an Anglican ministry in South Africa, my closest friends were a Mennonite mission couple. Afterwards I attended an ecumenical divinity school and I now work in an ecumenical theological education consortium. Each of these situations and relationships introduced me to different aspects of a shared Christian tradition and sometimes took me quite far from the tradition in which I was raised. In all these relationships, I managed to find a thread of commonality as well as new insights and practices that deepened my own faith.

The word for this is ecumenism, the term that describes relationships between Christians from different denominational backgrounds. Ecumenism is rooted in the same Greek word—*oikos*—that means household and which gives us the word economic as well. In this context, the etymology is a reminder that divided as Christians may be, we are all part of one household, the household of God. For many Christians, ecumenism is straightforwardly a Good Thing. After all, Jesus himself prayed for his followers "that they may all be one" (John 17:21). Ecumenical relationships seem a natural way of living out that prayer. But it is also possible for this to be a somewhat notional commitment. Sure, ecumenism is important, people might say, but we don't have time for that right now. The really important thing is actually topic X, where X might be social justice or Scriptural fidelity or evangelism and discipleship. Ecumenism can languish at the bottom of a list of priorities, hived off to worthy theological commissions that write reports few people read while everyone else gets on with what is deemed to be truly important.

In a crisis-shaped world, the future of many churches seems uncertain and fragile. It is easy to want to hunker down, to hang on to what we already have, and hope our congregations survive this storm. That would be a mistake. Instead, the church is called to embrace ecumenical relationship as central to its future. Yet in significant ways that ecumenical future needs to be different from our recent ecumenical past. Rather than focus on shared theological concerns, Christians need to focus on common action and common witness with other Christians who share life in our communities. To see a way forward, we first need to understand where we have come from.

* * *

The twentieth century has, in certain churchy circles, been called "the ecumenical century." In a way that was largely unprecedented in Christian history, many Christian churches sought closer relationship with one another through joint theological exploration and through negotiating reunion agreements in which they sought to become a single church. It is astonishing to read now both the depth of division between denominations—Christians not praying the Lord's Prayer together let alone receiving communion from another church—as well as the tremendous hope in mid-century when church leaders were quite convinced there would be a "coming great church" that brought all of Christ's followers together. It is, I believe, a beautiful vision. But it also did not happen—at least, not yet.

Broadly speaking, the ecumenical century can be divided into two halves. In the first half, running from about 1910 to the 1960s, the focus was on what was called "organic union." The goal was the formation of a single church entity out of two or more predecessor bodies. The most famous example of this was the Church of South India, formed in 1947 out of several denominations, including Anglican dioceses. By the early 1960s, virtually every Anglican church around the world was engaged in serious reunion negotiations with other Protestant denominations. In Canada, the United Church and the Anglican Church produced a draft Plan of Union for coming together in a single entity. The Episcopal Church worked on the Consultation on Church Union with Methodists, Presbyterians, and the United Church of Christ. The Church of England and the Methodist Church seriously considered reunion. Several denominations in Nigeria went through an extensive process that produced a plan for a single church. In virtually every instance, these negotiations failed to produce organic union. Sometimes the differences were theological. Sometimes they were about practical matters, like who would control the property or money. Sometimes the obstacles came from people who were committed to the preservation of existing structures and resisted reunion because of concerns about what would happen to their role in a new church.

The failure of many of these church union schemes coincided with a shift in emphasis in the second half of the ecumenical century, running from roughly the mid-1960s to the present. In this latter period, the focus was on "full communion." The goal was to maintain separate church entities but express a deeper relationship between them through such means as an interchange of members and ministers and, as the phrase implies, a sharing of Eucharistic fellowship. Almost immediately after the agreement with the Methodists (in England) and the United Church (in Canada) fell apart, Anglicans started pursuing theological reflection and agreement with Lutherans. This led in the early 1990s to the Porvoo Agreement that brought together the Anglican churches in the British Isles with some of the Lutheran churches in Europe. In the late 1990s and early 2000s, it led to full communion agreements between Lutherans and Anglicans in Canada and the United States. Lutheran clergy can be hired to work in Anglican and Episcopal congregations and vice versa with no trouble at all. But there are still distinct Anglican and Lutheran churches.

In the full communion era, the means of ecumenical advance has been the bilateral theological commission. Starting from the mid-1960s, Anglicans began to participate in a wide variety of these dialogues at both national and international levels. Sometimes, as was the case with the Lutherans, these commissions led to full communion agreements. When Anglicans and Lutherans began ecumenical conversation, it was clear that one of the obstacles to their relationship was the understanding of episcopal ministry: why do we have bishops and what do we mean by apostolic succession? A theological commission was appointed, hashed out the topic, and produced a report—in this case, *The Niagara Report*—that harmonized the differing understandings in a way that everyone agreed with.[1] It took more time to work out the final details but the theological commission opened a path to agreement. By contrast, Anglicans have been talking to Roman Catholics at both the national and international level since the late 1960s. This has produced some very fine theological reflection but has not brought the churches any closer to union or even the sharing of communion. Instead, these ecumenical reports and others like them from other theological commissions have piled up with little indication that they are having any discernible impact on the actual life of the church.

There was a significant difference between the organic union and full communion eras. The energy and impetus for the organic union movement came from the foreign missionary movement and the non-western church. In the classic telling of this story, western missionaries ended up overseas, realized how weak and paltry their efforts were, and came to understand that by cooperating with missionaries from other denominations they would be more effective. It was also a consistent testimony of non-western converts to Christianity that denominations were confusing, seemed like a western imposition, and should not be an obstacle to deeper relationship among Christians. The mission field became a natural place for experiment and the testing of new relationships. In 1913 in Kenya, two Anglican missionary bishops from England led an interdenominational communion service at the conclusion of a conference with Methodist and Presbyterian missionaries. Their action sparked intense opposition and controversy in England: how could Anglican bishops, who are supposed to believe in the importance of apostolic succession to ensure sacramental grace is present, offer communion to Christians from other denominations without apostolic succession? For the missionary bishops, it was a natural expression of their sense of colleagueship with their co-workers in the mission field. Later, the formation of the Church of South India also sparked remarkable vituperation and opposition in the Church of England, again tied to questions of church order and ministry. But the engine of organic union did its best to keep chugging along. At its best, the organic union movement kept its emphasis on the mission and witness of the church in a local area, engaged church members at all levels of the church, and tried to evolve structures that would serve Christians in their life of witness. It was undergirded by the belief that ecumenism and mission were two sides of the same coin and that the church's witness could only be strengthened by deeper ecumenical relationship. After all, when Jesus prayed for his followers to be one, he added "so that the world may believe" (John 17:21). The oneness of Jesus' followers was part of their witness to the world.

The full communion era, by contrast, has been dominated not by missionaries and non-western Christians but by leaders of churches in the western world. One moment that can be taken to mark the beginning of the full communion era is the visit that the Archbishop of Canterbury Michael Ramsey paid to the Vatican to visit Pope Paul VI in March 1966. It was the first time that an Archbishop of Canterbury met a pope in Rome since before the Reformation. The visit was part of the new openness to other Christians that Roman Catholics showed after the Second Vatican Council, and it led directly to the formation of the first Anglican Roman Catholic International Commission. But no one ever thought that Ramsey and Paul VI would preside over the bringing together of their churches. Organic union was always regarded as a distant goal. In the full communion era, the focus has been on theological reflection, not on integrating church structures to strengthen their witness to Christ.

As the focus of ecumenism has shifted toward church leaders and theological commissions, it has, at times, tended to abstract questions about the local life of the church and make them seem rather distant. A perennial refrain from the people who patiently engage in this important work of theological reflection is, "Why don't people pay attention to the work we do?" The answer may lie in the way in which the work has been done. By its nature, a report written by committee lacks urgency and immediacy. Its abstraction from local ministry means it is hard to put into action. One result is that ecumenism drops down the list of priorities in ministry. The reports are greeted with a collective shrug from the rest of the church who head off to focus on what they regard as more important.

Christians have generated immense and important theological reflection in the full communion era. We should give thanks for this. But the church in a crisis-shaped world cannot continue along this path. We need to re-center the importance of ecumenism in the life of the church in a way that has been lost in the full communion era. The way to do this is to return to the wisdom of the movement for organic union and reclaim a simple slogan: all in each place.

* * *

Some years ago I made a visit to Ecuador and met Nilton Giese, a Lutheran pastor and then the general secretary of the Latin American Council of Churches, a Protestant ecumenical organization. He described a contrast he detected between ecumenism in North America and ecumenism in Latin America. Northerners like me, he said, approached ecumenism by getting people together, talking about what we believe, and then trying to write down a shared understanding of our faith. It was a fine description of full communion ecumenism. By contrast, he said, "That's not what we do here. Here, we just start working in the world with other Christians. We figure out what we believe after we've been serving other people."

This comment reminded me of a refrain from the organic union era that is, in my view, simple and beautiful: all in each place. It comes from a longer statement from the 1961 meeting of the World Council of Churches and is sometimes called the greatest run-on sentence in ecumenical history:

> We believe that the unity which is both God's will and his gift to his Church is being made visible as all in each place who are baptized into Jesus Christ and confess him as Lord and Saviour are brought by the Holy Spirit into one fully committed fellowship, holding the one apostolic faith,

> preaching the one Gospel, breaking the one bread, joining in common prayer, and having a corporate life reaching out in witness and service to all and who at the same time are united with the whole Christian fellowship in all places and all ages in such wise that ministry and members are accepted by all, and that all can act and speak together as occasion requires for the tasks to which God calls his people.[2]

The sentence encompasses the totality of the Christian faith, including belief, worship, ministry, and service. In the phrase that is often pulled out of this sentence, the focus is ecumenical—"all"—and concrete and specific—"each place." The genius of "each place" is that it can be as narrow or expansive as it needs to be. It can mean a local neighborhood, a city, a province or state, or a country. It easily scales to fit the context. It calls on all Christians to join together for the sake of sharing the gospel in "witness and service" to others. It calls for Christians to be one so that, in Jesus' words, the world may believe.

The crises of our world make clear that Christians are in a missionary situation. The church has a gospel message to proclaim that needs to be heard—and it needs to be heard right in our midst. Yet church attendance is on the decline and the future of our institutions can seem uncertain. If we can see this clearly, we should understand that we are not that different from the scattered, disparate missionaries of generations past, trying to offer a Christian witness in a non-Christian environment. This situation should put us in the same mind as they once were: an ecumenical approach that prizes "all in each place" working together in witness and service. It is time to reclaim that old slogan and place our focus firmly on working together for the reign of God, beginning with the local and specific places in which our ministry is grounded.

It is important to be realistic. Although "all in each place" is a slogan of the organic union era, organic union is not going to happen overnight. There are too many vested interests and too long a history of suspicion and difficult relationships between church bodies. But we can start acting in ways as if it were already true. When we engage in ministry, we should reflexively look for Christians from other traditions to join with us. Many churches do this already, cooperating in food banks, homeless shelters, and other important ministries. But there remain many divisions. One of the most dispiriting recent experiences I've had occurred at that 2023 meeting of the General Synod of the Anglican Church of Canada. It was billed as a joint assembly with the Evangelical Lutheran Church in Canada, though since this was a full communion relationship some parts of our joint assembly were together and some were apart. In response to the murder of George Floyd in 2020, both churches had appointed commissions on anti-racism and both reported separately to their respective governing bodies. We were denied the opportunity to learn from each other's insights and to share the burden of this difficult and important work. I sat there imagining how much richer the work could have been if we could have mustered the courage to work together. And this was between two churches that declare themselves to be in full communion with each other. What would have been possible if we had managed to include other Christian traditions as well?

Beyond simply coordinating our work better, we also need to shift our identity. Rather than thinking of ourselves as a member of a denomination first—Anglican, Episcopal, Presbyterian, Methodist, whatever—the missionary situation in which we find ourselves means we need to start thinking of ourselves as Christians first. The primary part of our religious identity comes from a commitment to follow in the way of Jesus, not from any particular brand attached to it. It may seem odd to call a denominational identity a brand but that is precisely what it can become. I once attended an ecumenical conference in the United States in which the then-presiding bishop of the Evangelical Lutheran Church in America, Mark Hanson, spoke about his commitment to ecumenism. He then added, ruefully, "I can say that here but I have a meeting later this week with branding consultants to help build the image of my denomination." The pressures of institutional leadership and institutional survival are significant and one way to survive is for one's church to have an attractive "brand." But that is a death knell to hopes for ecumenical reunion. Rather than letting ourselves be weighed down by these denominational markers, we need to think of ourselves as Christians first. If we can do that, we can move toward a mindset that will point us toward "all in each place" ecumenism.

Encountering difference of any kind, including ecumenical difference, can raise concerns. One concern is often expressed like this: isn't it possible that if we engage ecumenically with other Christians, we will end up with a watered-down Christianity that emphasizes an unsatisfying least common denominator? This is an important question, though the fullness of the description of church that is offered in the longest run-on sentence in ecumenical history helps guard against that. More generally, the question reminds us that there is a paradoxical aspect to ecumenical encounter. On the one hand, ecumenism requires us to be constantly reaching out to Christians from different backgrounds and seeking new relationship. But there is another part to ecumenical encounter: we need to be deeply rooted in our own Christian tradition so as to offer the fullness of the gifts of our tradition to other Christians and ultimately the world around us. We need both to identify first as Christians while also understanding what it is that our tradition offers for the good of the whole. The most inspiring ecumenists are those who deeply know their own tradition and are eager to share its gifts with others, while also being open to receive the gifts that other traditions have to offer. Ecumenism requires both groundedness and openness, depth as well as reaching out. It is what has been described as a "roots down, walls down, bridges out" approach to inhabiting the Christian tradition.[3]

Ecumenism also requires faith and trust in the Holy Spirit who, through baptism, has brought together Christians from many different backgrounds into one body and who gives us the unity of that body as a gift and a witness to a divided world. Many times I have encountered Christians from other traditions and thought to myself something like, "Huh, not really sure what I have to receive here." But without fail I find that if I can stay in the encounter, I can find a glimmer (and usually much more than that) of that unity given to us in Christ.

The Holy Spirit continues to work in the church's midst in this crisis-shaped world, even as the institutional church seems weakened and uncertain. All in each place ecumenism prompts us to embrace our histories and our traditions, to reach out to others with the love of Jesus, and to move forward together into the future toward which the Spirit is leading us.

THESIS FIFTEEN

The Eucharist sets the agenda for the church

The COVID-19 pandemic put significant pressure on one of the central acts of Christian worship: the Eucharist. The taking and sharing of bread and wine as Jesus commanded be done in remembrance of him has in recent generations come to be understood as the central act of worship, the "principal act of Christian worship on the Lord's Day" as *The Book of Common Prayer* describes it.[1] But the Eucharist is an embodied and physical act. It requires the actual movement of one's body and the taking and consuming of bread (or wafers) and wine. When the pandemic made it impossible to gather in person, many churches were thrown into confusion: how could we worship without celebrating the Eucharist? A plethora of options emerged in response. Some churches live-streamed the worship service from the church and then encouraged a "drive-through" communion, in which the priest took the consecrated wafers outside for people to receive as they drove past. Others prioritized nonsacramental services of the word. Still others decided to encourage people to consume their own bread and wine at home as a quasi-sacramental act. Now, as in-person worship is re-established, the debates over virtual communion and spiritual communion seem to be fading along with memories of the pandemic.

What is still true, however, is that the Eucharist and its central place in the worshipping life of the church was under pressure well before the pandemic. This pressure came from two directions. First, to celebrate the Eucharist requires an ordained priest to be present.

But a growing number of churches are now struggling to have a priest every Sunday. To an extent, this has always been true in rural and remote regions. But the trend is now spreading to more populated areas. As churches struggle financially, it is harder and harder to afford a full-time clergy person who can reliably be present every Sunday. Some churches join together with others to afford a full-time person but that person has to split their time between multiple congregations and is often unable to celebrate the Eucharist every Sunday in each church. Other churches rely on reserved sacrament—bread and wine consecrated elsewhere and brought to them by a lay person or a deacon. Some churches ordain clergy whose chief source of income is elsewhere than the church. Moreover, there are simply fewer clergy than there have been in the past. The Evangelical Lutheran Church in Canada has begun to experiment with having lay people preside at sacramental services, arguing that this is an appropriate and contextual response to the needs of congregations in rural parts of the country.

Another pressure on the Eucharist comes from considering who is receiving it. Historically, many Christians have understood that baptism is a necessary precondition to the reception of the Eucharist. That's why the baptism service precedes the Eucharist service in *The Book of Common Prayer* and why many newer church buildings have oriented themselves with a baptismal font near the entrance and an altar farther away. One passes through the font to reach the altar. Much of this thinking originated at a time in which the church could reasonably assume that most people were baptized as infants. That no longer holds true. Western societies are more pluralistic and more secular. That means that there are more people who may have grown up in a faith other than Christianity, or not grown up in a faith at all. This has led to considerable and at times quite bitter debate in some parts of the church. In Anglican and Episcopal churches, the official teaching remains that baptism is to precede Eucharist but many congregations have adopted a practice of "open communion," that is, inviting all people regardless of their background to the communion rail. It is said to be a practice that reflects the indiscriminate hospitality of Jesus. It is also said to be a practice that offends against the central theological presuppositions that gave rise to *The Book of Common Prayer*. I raise this not to discuss the merits of this debate but to note that it is a debate that results from the centrality of the Eucharist. If the church were celebrating the Eucharist less frequently, these considerations would be considerably lessened.

As I draw these theses to a conclusion, I end with the Eucharist. The Eucharist makes clear that as the church faces a crisis-shaped world, it is itself beset by challenges including over this central act. Having for several generations declared the Eucharist to be its "principal act" of worship, many churches now find they can no longer sustain this commitment as they once did. Yet if we delve more deeply into the Eucharist, we can find a way forward both for the church and for its mission and witness in the world.

* * *

As they were for the broader western world, the 1960s were a time of considerable change for the church. This is perhaps most evident in the changing understanding of the word "mission." Mission has a mixed legacy for many churches. European missionaries who traveled to Asia, Africa, or other parts of the world were, for a time, seen as heroes of the faith. But in the wake of the Second World War, amid the decolonization of European empires, many missionaries came to a new understanding of their role—and they didn't terribly like it. They began to see the way in which the act of mission had been closely tied up in colonial power, imperialism, and racist understandings of human difference. As part of their effort to distance themselves from this past legacy, they developed a new understanding: mission belonged to God, not the church. It was God who was acting in the world and God's action always pointed in the direction of God's kingdom, a kingdom of *shalom* or peace, wholeness, and welfare for all. If this was the case, then the goal of mission needed to change. Rather than seeing the goal of mission as the building up of more churches, the goal of mission now became to work for the realization of God's kingdom in the world. This changed how Christians understood God's action. Rather than understanding God acting through the church and then the church acting in the world, God was now understood to be acting first in the world. The church needed to figure out where that was and join in. In the summer of 1968, not long after their intended keynote speaker Martin Luther King, Jr. had been assassinated and in the midst of significant social turmoil, the General Assembly of the World Council of Churches met in Sweden. The meeting is remembered for its insistence on the need for revolutionary activism by Christians. This agenda is often remembered by the phrase "the world sets the agenda for the church." In other words, Christians should take their cues from what is happening in the world.

The implications of this shift were profound. It encouraged more Christians to become engaged in social justice and work for societal transformation as they came to understand this as part of their Christian calling. While there was much to praise in these developments, there were further developments that were not always so welcome. If what was important was working to build the kingdom of God in the world and not what was happening in the church, then perhaps the church could be sidelined or dispensed with altogether. Who needed its archaic traditions and outdated rites when there were so many more pressing issues of justice to be working on? If it was the world that set the agenda and it seemed like the church was not supporting that agenda quickly or fully enough, then why not just leave behind the church altogether? The result is what has been described as the secularization of mission. For some Christians, mission and social transformation came to be synonymous. It became unclear what unique value the Christian gospel had to add.[2]

It was in this same period that Christians around the world were engaged in a renewal of their liturgies that led to the profound statements about Eucharistic centrality that so many Episcopalians, Anglicans, and other Protestants take for granted today. This renewal was grounded in the belief that what happens in the church is central to how Christians understand God's actions in the world. It is in the Eucharist that Christians perceive the reign of God and are formed to be God's people. At one and the same time, many Christians were concluding both that what took place in church—the Eucharist—was of vital importance and that the real meaning of Christian action—mission—was found in the world. The 1960s and 1970s were a period in which church membership for mainline Protestants peaked in the western world before beginning the gradual and then more rapid decline that is familiar today. A church that could not in its theology make up its mind about whether what happened in the church was important or not was a church that would struggle to articulate a rationale for ongoing membership.

This history matters because it continues to shape the church today. On the one hand, there are church communities that are driven to make vitally needed change in the world. On the other hand, these same church communities are increasingly burdened by a model of worship—Eucharistic centrality—that is under considerable pressure. In searching for ways to reconcile the injustice of the world with the sacramental practice that has formed me since childhood I found my way to a new understanding: it is not the world that sets the agenda for the church, nor is it the church that sets the agenda for the world. Rather, the Eucharist sets the agenda for the church and its part in the mission of God. In this idea, I believe, lies a path through a difficult conflict and, more significantly, into renewed Christian witness in the world.

* * *

One of the major insights in making the Eucharist central to liturgical celebration was the idea that the Eucharist is a series of actions. In the same way that the gospels tell us Jesus took bread, gave thanks, broke it, and gave it to his disciples, the Eucharistic prayer needed to be marked by the same actions. As the service was reconceived, it was these actions that gave shape to the central prayer: taking bread on the altar, giving thanks to God, breaking it, and then giving it.[3]

But it is not just the Eucharistic prayer that is a collection of actions. The entirety of the Eucharistic liturgy, from the opening of the service to the dismissal, is a series of actions that collectively create the liturgy. The community gathers before God. It reads and listens to Scripture as a community. The people declare their faith, confess sin, pass peace, and make an offering of our gifts to God. The community remembers God's saving action in the Eucharistic prayer, gives thank for Christ's death and resurrection, and prays for God's kingdom to come. Each of these actions takes place inside the church building. What I have begun to realize is that each of these actions can also take place outside the context of a Eucharistic liturgy, indeed outside of a church building altogether. These actions can provide a shape for my living in the world.

Take peace-passing first. When I was growing up in church, I recall the passing of the peace as being akin to the seventh-inning stretch of a baseball game: a time to greet those around me, ask my parents how much time was left in the service, and maybe pretend I had to go to the bathroom so I could swing by the parlor to see if I could nab an early coffee hour treat. Peace passing is rooted in a couple of different parts of the Bible, including Paul's admonition to great one another with a "holy kiss" (Rom. 16:16). The Biblical warrant I am always drawn to comes from Jesus' Sermon on the Mount: "So when you are offering your gift at the altar, if you remember that your brother or sister has something against you, leave your gift there before the altar and go; first be reconciled to your brother or sister, and then come and offer your gift" (Matt. 5:23–24). Jesus tells us that if we are not reconciled with one another, then in a very real way our actions at the altar lack meaning and substance. Reconciliation is an important, if troubled, word for Christians. It is often used to structure the church's response to societal problems. If we are serious about being peace-passers—and the centrality of the Eucharist would seem to indicate that we are—then this action can provide an orientation that guides our life together outside the church as well by prompting some helpful questions. If we take peace-passing seriously, we should be asking: With whom in this congregation am I trying to avoid passing the peace? With whom do I genuinely need to seek reconciliation? Does it feel particularly false with anyone when I say, "Peace be with you"? More importantly, we should be asking ourselves: who is not in this congregation? With whom am I missing opportunities for reconciliation because they are not in this Eucharistic community?

This last question can help offer guidance and direction for our lives as Christians in the world. The passing of the peace reminds me that I need to leave the church to seek the fullness of reconciliation to which I, as a Christian, am called, and find these relationships outside the church doors as well. If I remember my calling to be a peace passer and especially to be a peace passer with those who are not in my congregation, it will drive me out into the world to seek new relationship with those who are different from me. The Eucharist—specifically the action of passing the peace—will have set the agenda for my life as a Christian in the world. These questions cannot and should not just be asked by individual Christians, of course, but by whole congregations. If a group of people from similar backgrounds is celebrating the Eucharist together, the calling of the Eucharist should impel them to ask who is missing and what steps they need to take in the world to broaden their Eucharistic community and seek peace with all.

Here's another example. Most Eucharistic liturgies contain a confession of sin, accompanied by an absolution of those same sins and a promise of God's mercy, peace, and forgiveness. The Christian belief is that confession and absolution lead then to amendment of life. Having become aware of our sin, our call is, by God's grace, to change our life. Sin may not be a popular word in some corners of the church or world, but it remains an ever-present reality. All of us, I believe, have some innate understanding of what sin is and what wrong is. What we constantly need to be reminded of is that through Jesus these sins are forgiven.

What many Christians also increasingly recognize is that sin is not just individual—I yelled at my children, I fought with my spouse—but also structural. All of us live in a fallen world and the sinfulness of humanity has become part of the structures of this fallen world. Racism is a structural sin, for instance, in the way that it structures opportunities and outcomes for some people in unjust and undeserved fashion. Our economic system, as we have seen, oppresses the poor and propounds values antithetical to Christianity. It too is an example of structural sin. Indeed, the essential truth of our crisis-shaped world is that we all live in and participate in structures of sin, structures that point us away from the fullness of God's vision for human life and the whole created order. Responding to these structures can and should be part of the life and work of Christians in the world. But in my experience, they are rarely brought to mind by the prayer of confession in the Eucharist.

What would happen if we let the action of confession set the agenda for our witness in the world? This is a hard thing to write about because writing about one's own sin is either painful or puts me at risk of looking sanctimonious. But let me offer three examples in which I have begun to take the practice of confession with me into the world. When I pump gas in my car, I know that I am participating in an energy system that is harming the environment my children and grandchildren will inherit. I offer a prayer of repentance in this moment. When I eat a meal prepared in a way that I know was harmful to the earth or the animals that are part of God's creation, I offer not simply a prayer of thanksgiving but also a prayer of confession for the way in which the meal is the result of a broken relationship with God's creation. When I order a new book online, I confess that I am supporting companies whose commitment to fair labor practices or public, shared spaces I question.

Do any of these confessions have an impact? I still need to drive. I still need to eat. I sure like buying new books. But it is possible to detect a shift in my life. I think much more deliberately about my use of the car and ways in which I can use alternative transportation strategies. I think much more clearly about where my food comes from and the ways in which I am connected with those places, in both unjust and, I hope, more just fashions. I try to plan my book-buying in advance so I can build in the lag time needed to get it at a bookstore with a more demonstrated commitment to the common good. My life has not abruptly changed. I am still part of many structures of sin. But on some days I can see the ways in which the trajectory of my life is moving closer toward the wholeness of life that characterizes the reign of God. Perhaps some of these alternative strategies are more available to me than others. I live in a city with excellent public transit, for instance, and great bike lanes. That's true and serves as a reminder of how all-encompassing structures of sin can be. But we should not underestimate the power of God's absolving grace to transform individual lives and structures.

Here is a final example. There is a part of every Eucharistic prayer that liturgical scholars call the *anamnesis*, a Greek word often translated as "remembering." Reasonable people differ on where precisely in the prayer this is found, but it is there when the prayer remembers all that God has done for us as well as in summation language like this: "Remembering now his work of redemption, and offering to you this sacrifice of thanksgiving, we celebrate his death and resurrection, as we await the day of his coming."[4] We remember God's saving action through history and above all in Jesus Christ. We need to do this every time we celebrate the Eucharist because we are in danger of forgetting. But what this also makes clear is that remembering is not simply an action that looks backwards. Remembering is an eschatological action: it situates us in our present moment while also pointing us forward. This should be clear to anyone who pays attention to politics. I live in Quebec, where the slogan on the license plates is *je me souviens*, literally "I remember." By not specifying what precisely is being remembered, it unites us as people who remember in the present moment, looking both to the past and to the future as we do. The slogan "Make America Great Again" is a kind of politicized remembering as well. It recalls a past to shape a present and provide guidance for a future. What we choose to remember forms us into who we are, both as individuals and as communities. In the Eucharist, the act of remembering enables the community to live with hope and confidence, knowing that Christ will come again, judgments will be made right, and all will be restored in right relationship. Remembering situates us on the eschatological timeline that is so important for Christian witness in a crisis-shaped world.

But remembering happens not just in churches. In my mind, a word closely related to remembering is attentiveness, a word I have already explored at length. In the Eucharist, we remember how God was attentive to us. But we can extend that attention to others as well, in the same way that Jesus reached out to others. When the Eucharist centers the importance of remembering for me, I can—at my best—take this orientation toward remembering outside of church. I am drawn to recall, give heed to, and be attentive to those who are often ignored or forgotten.

These three examples—peace-passing, confession and absolution, and remembering—are all offered as demonstrations of the ways in which the Eucharist can set the agenda for Christians in the world. There are many more actions in the Eucharist and many more fertile areas for reflection and Christian activity. But the broader point remains. As a result of changes over recent generations, the Eucharist is seen as central to the life of the church, and the church understands its calling outside its doors as well. By taking the Eucharist and its actions outside the church we can allow the Eucharist to set the agenda. If we see this clearly, we can see the ways in which Christian witness can begin to offer a faithful, credible, and hopeful response to the needs of a crisis-shaped world.

CONCLUSION

In November 1968, the theologian Donald MacKinnon delivered a lecture in Westminster Abbey. It was an odd juxtaposition. MacKinnon had been born in the Scottish Highlands and was a member of the Scottish Episcopal Church, a small denomination in a nation where the Reformed Christian tradition was dominant. Westminster Abbey is at the heart of the English state and the English church, directly across from the Houses of Parliament and not far from Buckingham Palace. MacKinnon, a layman and professor at Cambridge University, had cultivated a reputation as an eccentric even by the standards of Cambridge. Westminster Abbey is a place of buttoned-down propriety and is served by a small army of priests. Most of all, Westminster Abbey is the heart of establishment in the Church of England. The Abbey is directly under the authority of the English sovereign. It is the place where monarchs are crowned and buried, and heirs to the throne married. It embodies the melding of spiritual and temporal authority in the Church of England in which bishops sit in the House of Lords and the Archbishop of Canterbury ranks ahead of the prime minister. The Church of England is an established church, and no place better represents this fact than Westminster Abbey.

MacKinnon's lecture, titled "Kenosis and Establishment," took direct aim at the legacy and reality of establishment. *Kenosis* is a Greek word used in the New Testament to refer to the "self-emptying" of Christ in the Incarnation and on the cross (Phil. 2:5–11). Within the walls of Westminster Abbey, MacKinnon proclaimed that a new era of the church was arriving, one in which it could no longer expect that its political and societal connections would secure its place or legitimacy in the world. Rather, he said, the church should be open to and embrace what could be possible if it left those privileges behind. Establishment had led the church astray, MacKinnon argued, and now society was leaving the church behind. The result was an opportunity for Christian witness to return to the strange, difficult, and ultimately beautiful mystery at the heart of the gospel. But MacKinnon also realized it would not be easy to get from the current position of establishment to the emerging position of *kenosis*. Toward the end of his lecture, he said:

> [T]he issue of *kenosis* and establishment is, in the end, an issue of spirituality. To live as a Christian in the world today is necessarily to live an exposed life; it is to be stripped of the kind of security that tradition. . .easily bestows. We deceive ourselves if we suppose that we do not seek to hide ourselves away from the kind of exposure to which I am referring. To do so might quite properly be thought the besetting sin of the characteristically Anglican ethos, a cultivated avoidance of extremes. And whether we like it or not, today we do live in an extreme situation.[1]

Whether legally established, as in England, or not, as in the United States, Scotland, Canada, and elsewhere, many Anglicans and Episcopalians have long held tightly to the kind of security and privilege that is provided by a building, a professional and well-compensated clergy person, and a respectable place in society. Many of the people who attend these churches have likewise been able to occupy a privileged societal position thanks to their education, income, and connections. What we might call the ethos of establishment has long permeated Anglican witness. As I described in the introduction and elsewhere in this book, throughout the decades after the Second World War, the rule of law, steadily rising home values, and a growing economy created a bubble of contentment for white, well-educated people in the North Atlantic world and led to the "end of history" environment in which I was raised. This security and privilege is an echo of this ethos. For both mainline Protestant churches and for many of their members, it has made it possible to put off reckoning with the implications of MacKinnon's insight and to adopt only rhetorically, if at all, the *kenosis* that Christ took on and which the New Testament urges on his followers.

But now, at different paces and in different ways, uncertainty and weakness are being forced upon our churches, our institutions, and ourselves, even as the gathering crises of our world make the urgency of Christian witness palpable. As climate change continues to intensify it is becoming impossible to avoid its impacts: wildfire smoke, floods, heat waves, too-warm winters, and so much more. The ongoing movement of people around the world, including climate refugees fleeing flooding or wildfire in the United States and Canada, means that all of us are being forced to come to terms with the challenges that people in other parts of the world confront. Greater attention to Indigenous peoples in North America means a growing recognition that these challenges and others are shared by people on whose land our forebears unjustly settled. Intensifying inequality and commodification rooted in a neoliberal economic model make employment more precarious for a greater percentage of the population and put previously necessary goods like housing further out of reach. If we needed any further indication, the COVID-19 pandemic revealed that all of us are vulnerable to sudden and unplanned disruption. Whether we like it or not, security and long-held privilege are under threat for more and more people. Those with resources will be able to forestall the negative impacts for longer than those without but the logic of a crisis-shaped world is remorseless.

In writing these theses, I have been continually struck by—and often stuck on—what feels like the great gap between the transcendent mystery and potential of the Christian gospel to speak to this moment of human history and the fragility of the church in a crisis-shaped world. Many churches I know feel as if they are focused entirely on the next step that leads not to their thriving but to their survival. I know of many wonderful ministries and programs but it does not always seem as if they get to the heart of the crises that shape human society. In these theses, I have been trying to encourage Christians to "lift up their eyes" and understand the broader context in which we live and how the gospel message speaks directly to this moment. Still, I know that many people who read these theses will by this point be asking a question like this: What does this all mean for my congregation? How can this help us survive? In other words: What is the church going to look like as we move forward in a world in polycrisis?

In response, I can only but point to MacKinnon's words. What is most needed is not a new program or a new plan. Rather, what is needed is a spirituality that allows us to be and to be present in this time of polycrisis in a way that is confident, attentive, and hopeful. That spirituality will be one that recognizes the opportunities that flow from leaving behind the privilege and connection which has so shaped much of Christian witness for generations. If we can see this moment truly for what it is—both in the church and in the world the church inhabits—there is tremendous potential. Christians in the twenty-first century are faithful to the same God that Christians have been faithful to across these last millennia of Christian history. But as has been true at many previous points in that history, in order to stay faithful to that unchanging God, the church has sometimes needed to change. The result may be a community that is different from what we once knew but still faithful to the same God. What could that community look like?

There is not one shape of church that is best suited for a crisis-shaped world. Different contexts will lead to different expressions of Christianity that are faithful to the same gospel. Still, it will not come as a surprise if I say that this emerging faith will reverse some of the trends of mainline Protestant theology in recent generations and become more apocalyptic and eschatological. Jesus himself understood that the kingdoms of this world are powerful and obstruct the coming of the reign of God. The same needs to be true for us. The Christian gospel is not the only power that is seeking to form and shape people in this world. We are better off for stating this fact openly. Christians need to develop the ability to see with an apocalyptic clarity, hold fast to those truths that are revealed, and live confidently in hope of God's ongoing and future action.

That will likely lead us to recognize how our churches, our people, and our very selves have become entangled in these powers and distracted from the reign of God. All of us are subject to these pressures. No less than any other organization, churches have succumbed at times to the values of a neoliberal economic model or ignored their relationships in the broader community of creation. Still, we may find that the pressures the churches are under right now can help lead to new clarity of sight. Take, as just one example, the relationship that church communities have with their buildings. In the contexts with which I am most familiar, the pandemic has only accelerated trends that were already in place. Some congregations are selling their buildings, in some cases to rent back part of the space or in others to leave the building behind entirely. This decision can bring with it lots of emotion and is a decision that is not made lightly. Buildings are cherished places, to me as much as to anyone else. But they can also come to occupy a too central place in the minds of some congregations, functioning as a kind of power that can distract from the witness of the community. As we learn more about congregations that are exploring a new relationship with their building and their place, we are seeing that in some instances letting go of a building that may have consumed tremendous amounts of time and energy can be immensely liberating, freeing congregations to dream of new ways to offer common worship, common ground, and common service to the world around them. We need to stop thinking that when a church congregation decides to sell its building that means the congregation has somehow "failed." It has not. It has just reached another point in its witness.

In a crisis-shaped world, the basic markers of Christian identity and faith provide a resource for Christians to draw on. In previous theses, I suggested how some of these ideas, like attentiveness, enoughness, or mercy, to name just a few, still speak to us today. Likewise, in the final thesis I illustrated how the practice of the Eucharist can be a marker that guides life outside the church walls. To take time to give thanks—the literal meaning of the word eucharist—for what God has done in and through Jesus Christ and to recognize the gifts God has given to us and offer them back to God are profoundly important steps in acknowledging God's presence and saving power in this world. It is fair to say that the pressures of the world do not often allow much time for delight or thanksgiving. There remains so much more space for creative interpretations and insights from the inheritance of the Christian faith.

When I look back over the Bible stories I've referred to in these theses, I am drawn to how frequently people in those stories must have been afraid: a bunch of recently freed slaves wandering in the wilderness not sure where their next meal is going to come from or if their leader really knows where they are going; a wounded man by the side of the road thinking he is going to die and not sure why that strange Samaritan is approaching him; a bunch of disciples huddled in an upper room, their teacher apparently dead, and not sure if they will be the next to hang on a cross. Time and again, the message of God to fearful people is, in one way or another, simply this: "fear not"—and then, "I am with you."

Many of us who once lived with certainty are now realizing we need to live with uncertainty—about our place in the world, about the future, about our churches. This can be challenging, overwhelming, and fear-inducing. It can make us think we have failed or that we should just give up. But in the midst of this uncertainty, God's faithfulness remains steadfast even as our own ways of following God change. In that truth, we can find courage and not fear. God is with us even now in the midst of this crisis-shaped world.

ACKNOWLEDGMENTS

I wrote this book while serving as principal of Montreal Diocesan Theological College. I have dedicated this book to the "Dio" community—staff and faculty colleagues, governors, and above all my stimulating and challenging students—as a token of my thanks for all they have given me over these years of change and transformation for me and for the college. Many of these ideas were first explored and tested with this community of people who embody what it means to be faithful, creative, and hopeful.

This book began as a few thoughts about the church after the COVID-19 pandemic. In conversation with friends and colleagues, however, I was encouraged to set these thoughts within the broader frame of crisis and think more broadly than simply the church. I am immensely grateful for this prodding which has made this a much stronger book. A wide range of people in and beyond Montreal have served as conversation partners for these ideas. This includes Jenna Smith, Jeffrey Metcalfe, Ross Kane, Martha Tatarnic, Jordan Ware, Iain Luke, Grayhame Boycott, and Rhonda Waters. In addition to being conversation partners Jessica Stilwell, Scott MacDougall, Giuseppe Gagliano, Chris Barrigar, Maylanne Maybee, Ian Douglas, and Jen Bourque read and commented on chapters or the full text. Anne Privett also read the text and, at a crucial moment, reminded me of Luther's *incurvatus in se* and started me thinking about body posture in the attention economy and in the garden. I was also able to test ideas in invitations to address, variously, the Society of Catholic Priests, the Diocese of Western Massachusetts, and the Diocese of Quebec, and was grateful for feedback from those events. I am immensely grateful for the people of Waswanipi who have welcomed my students and me on a couple of occasions, notably Cliff Dee and his congregation. I am also grateful to Allan Saganash for sharing his wisdom at such length and with such generosity.

I have previously explored some of the ideas in this book in other venues. This includes "The Deified Market," in the *Anglican Theological Review* 101.2 (2019); "Shall All Be Well? Living in Hope During a Pandemic," in the *Christian Century* 137.16 (29 July 2020); "Catholicity," in *Saving Words: 20 Redemptive Words Worth Rescuing*, edited by Joe Pagano and Amy Richter (Cascade Press, 2022); "The Promise of Place: Shaping a Local Anglican Response to Global Realities" in *Partnerships as Mission: Essays in Memory of Ellie Johnson*, edited by Kenneth Gray and Maylanne Maybee (Cascade Press, 2023); and "Anglican Theology in the Midst of a Migration Crisis," in the *Journal of Anglican Studies* 17.1 (2019). All material in this book has been reworked and rewritten from these initial publications. My approach to "all in each place" ecumenism was first developed in a series of online essays I wrote in anticipation of the 2023 General Synod of the Anglican Church of Canada and posted on Medium. As I was completing this book, my essay "Place and Land in Anglican Theology: Intercultural Theology in a Global World" was published in the *Anglican Theological Review* 106.1 (2024) and represents a parallel and fuller development of ideas in this book.

I have again enjoyed my experience of working with the team at Church Publishing. Thank you as well to you, the reader, for engaging in the market economy by purchasing this book and ensuring that there continues to be a viable market in the church for the book-length articulation of ideas. I am convinced that this is vital to the continued flourishing of the church. Have you considered buying a separate copy for a friend?

In writing this book, I have often felt that several threads that have long worked their way through my life are coming together. One is my love for language and etymology, nurtured by a series of talented Latin, Greek, and Hebrew teachers, notably Theresa Bimbane,

James Bridgman, Beert Verstraete and Timothy Ashley. Another is my connection to St. John's Episcopal Church in Northampton, Massachusetts where I was raised. It is the same church in which Willliam Stringfellow was raised, though we were about fifty years apart. I attended Sunday School in the Bayne parlor, named for former rector Stephen Bayne. Stringfellow went on to be a lawyer, activist, and theologian. Bayne went on to be a mid-century bishop and global church leader. Though I do not quote either directly in this book, I think often of both these men and our shared connection to St. John's. To Stringfellow, I owe a debt of thinking apocalyptically and writing as clearly and directly as possible from a position, I hope, of deep grounding in a sacramental expression of the Christian gospel. To Bayne, I owe the constant reminder that God is acting even now in the world and that the Christian gospel speaks clearly to the concerns of our present moment, however different our moment may be from his. In my time at St. John's and from a young age, Jim Munroe formed me in a gospel of grace and mercy that I have tried never to lose sight of, even if I was not always aware of it at the time.

Debbie keeps me grounded in the reality of congregational ministry and continues to support me in a vocation that keeps me glued to a computer screen or book and lost in thought far more regularly than she would prefer. I could not do this without her support and partnership on this journey.

NOTES

Introduction: Polycrisis and Christian Witness

1. There are few good words to refer to regions of the world. In this book, I use "western," "Euro-Atlantic," and "North Atlantic" interchangeably to refer to the United States, Canada, and western Europe, cognizant of the deficiencies of each of these phrases.
2. David Leonhardt, *Ours Was the Shining Future: The Story of the American Dream* (New York: Random House, 2023).
3. Adam Tooze, "Welcome to the world of the polycrisis," *Financial Times* October 29, 2022: 11. A related word is permacrisis, which is also in current use, and refers to a similar idea.
4. Other accessible books, both recent and not, that I have found helpful in offering a Christian response to this moment of crisis include Mary Jo Leddy, *Say to the Darkness, We Beg to Differ* (Toronto: Lester & Orpen Dennys, 1990), Kenneth Leech, *The Sky is Red: Discerning the Signs of the Times* (London: Darton Longman & Todd, 2003), Fred Bahnson and Norman Wirzba, *Making Peace with the Land: God's Call to Reconcile with Creation* (Downers Grove, IL: IVP Books, 2012), Stephanie Spellers, *Church Cracked Open: Disruption, Decline, and New Hope for Beloved Community* (New York: Church Publishing, 2021), and Tim Dickau, *Forming Christian Communities in a Secular Age: Recovering Humility and Hope* (Toronto: Tyndale Academic Press, 2021).
5. Membership and average attendance figures for the Episcopal Church are available online: https://generalconvention.org/membership-average-attendance/. The Anglican Church of Canada report is referenced in Tali Folkins, "Gone by 2040?" *Anglican Journal* January 6, 2020. Online at https://anglicanjournal.com/gone-by-2040/. The statistics from 2019 to 2022 are available in "Statistics Report to General Synod 2023," available online at https://assembly.anglicanlutheran.ca/wp-content/uploads/4b-Report-006-Appendix-B-Statistics-Report.pdf.

Thesis 1 A crisis-shaped world requires apocalyptic clarity

1. Martin Luther King, Jr. "Remaining Awake Through a Great Revolution," sermon delivered March 31, 1968, compiled in *A Testament of Hope: The*

Essential Writings and Speeches of Martin Luther King, Jr., ed. James M. Washington (New York: HarperOne, 1986), 268–278.
2. D.S. Russell, *The Method and Message of Jewish Apocalyptic* (London: SCM Press, 1964), 17.
3. A recent expression of this line of thinking is Steven Charleston, *We Survived the End of the World: Lessons from Native America on Apocalypse and Hope* (Minneapolis, MN: Broadleaf Books, 2023).

Thesis 2 Economic structures are the greatest obstacle to Christian witness

1. Emily Guendelsberger, *On the Clock: What Low-Wage Work Did to Me and How It Drives America Insane* (New York: Little, Brown and Company, 2019), 256. Italics in the original.
2. Elizabeth Warren and Amelia Warren Tyagi, *The Two-Income Trap: Why Middle-Class Mothers and Fathers Are Going Broke* (New York: Basic Books, 2003).
3. I have drawn this recapitulation of economic history from several sources. A very useful and accessible recent overview of this period is Gary Gerstle, *The Rise and Fall of the Neoliberal Order: America and the World in the Free Market Era* (New York: Oxford University Press, 2022).
4. Reagan likely did not originate these words but he used them at a press conference on August 12, 1986. Transcript available online at https://www.reaganlibrary.gov/archives/speech/presidents-news-conference-23.
5. Margaret Thatcher, "Interview for 'Woman's Own' ('No Such Thing as Society')," 1987. Available online from the Margaret Thatcher Foundation at https://www.margaretthatcher.org/document/106689.
6. Clinton made this comment in his 1996 State of the Union address. Available online at https://clintonwhitehouse4.archives.gov/WH/New/other/sotu.html.
7. Francis Fukuyama, *The End of History and the Last Man* (New York: Free Press, 1992).
8. Michael J. Sandel, *What Money Can't Buy: The Moral Limits of Markets* (New York: Penguin Books, 2012), 10–11.
9. Francis, *Evangelii Gaudium: The Joy of the Gospel*, November 2013, para. 55. Available online at https://www.vatican.va/content/francesco/en/apost_exhortations/documents/papa-francesco_esortazione-ap_20131124_evangelii-gaudium.html.

10. Justin Welby, *Dethroning Mammon: Making Money Serve Grace* (New York: Bloomsbury, 2016).
11. The parallels between Christianity and a market-based religion are explored at greater length in Scott W. Gustafson, *At the Altar of Wall Street: The Rituals, Myths, Theologies, Sacraments, and Mission of the Religion Known as the Modern Global Economy* (Grand Rapids, MI: Eerdmans, 2015) and Harvey Cox, *The Market as God* (Cambridge, MA: Harvard University Press, 2016).

Thesis 3 Christian formation is not failing. It's being defeated

1. Just in the field of African religion, the literature on religious change is considerable. Two representative works are Robin Horton, "African Conversion," *Africa* 41.2 (1971): 85–108 and J.D.Y. Peel, *Religious Encounter and the Making of the Yoruba* (Indianapolis: Indiana University Press, 2000).
2. I have provided an extended study of one such example of this in *Christianity and Catastrophe in South Sudan: Civil War, Migration, and the Rise of Dinka Anglicanism* (Waco, TX: Baylor University Press, 2018).
3. James K. A. Smith, *You Are What You Love: The Spiritual Power of Habit* (Grand Rapids, MI: Brazos Press, 2016), 37.

Thesis 4 Christians offer attentiveness to a distracted people

1. There are various studies on this. These figures come from Reviews .org, "Cell phone usage statistics," July 21, 2023, https://www.reviews .org/mobile/cell-phone-addiction/.
2. Pope Francis, *Fratelli Tutti: On Fraternity and Social Friendship*, October 2020, para. 30. Available online at https://www.vatican.va /content/francesco/en/encyclicals/documents/papa-francesco_20201003 _enciclica-fratelli-tutti.html.
3. The prayer is one of the collects for mission in the Morning Prayer service. *The Book of Common Prayer and Administration of the Sacraments and Other Rites and Ceremonies of the Church* (New York: Church Hymnal Corporation, 1979), 101.
4. Martin Luther, *Lectures on Romans*, ed. and translated by Wilhelm Pauck (Louisville, KY: Westminster John Knox Press, 2006/1961), 159.

Thesis 5 Enough is a response to a world of more

1. Justin Welby, *Dethroning Mammon: Making Money Serve Grace* (New York: Bloomsbury, 2016), 1.

2. Jimmy Carter, "Crisis of Confidence," delivered July 15, 1979. Available online at https://www.pbs.org/wgbh/americanexperience/features/carter-crisis/.
3. In this section, I have drawn on J.B. MacKinnon, *The Day the World Stops Shopping* (New York: HarperCollins, 2021).
4. I am indebted to Ellen Davis' reading of this passage in *Scripture, Culture, and Agriculture: An Agrarian Reading of the Bible* (Cambridge: Cambridge University Press, 2009), 66–79.
5. The phrase appeared in the communion prayer in *The Book of Common Prayer* produced by Archbishop of Canterbury Thomas Cranmer in 1549 and has appeared in many versions since.

Thesis 6 The catholicity of the Christian community is its response to a globally-connected world

1. Cyril of Jerusalem, *Catechetical Lecture 18*, para 23. In *The Works of Saint Cyril of Jerusalem: Volume 2*, trans. by Leo McCauley and Anthony A. Stephenson (Washington, D.C.: The Catholic University of America Press, 1970), 132.
2. Rowan Williams, "One Holy Catholic and Apostolic Church: Archbishop's Address to the 3rd Global South to South Encounter Ain al Sukhna, Egypt," October 28, 2005. Available online at http://aoc2013.brix.fatbeehive.com/articles.php/1675/one-holy-catholic-and-apostolic-church.

Thesis 7 In an angry world, the Christian answer is mercy.

1. Walter Wink, *The Powers That Be: Theology for a New Millennium* (New York: Galilee Doubleday, 1998), 42–62.

Thesis 8 Christian witness is rooted in hope—even if we don't want it to be.

1. Solastalgia was coined by the Australian philosopher Glenn Albrecht in 2005. He develops this idea at greater length in his book *Earth Emotions: New Words for a New World* (Ithaca, NY: Cornell University Press, 2019).
2. *The Hymnal 1982* (New York: Church Hymnal Corporation, 1985), #89 and #90.
3. *The Book of Common Prayer and Administration of the Sacraments and Other Rites and Ceremonies of the Church* (New York: Church Hymnal Corporation, 1979), 861.

4. P.D. James, *The Children of Men* (New York: Alfred A. Knopf, 1993), 98. Originally published in 1992 in London by Faber and Faber.
5. James, *The Children of Men*, 75.
6. James, *The Children of Men*, 110.

Thesis 9 Place matters: Christian witness begins in particular and specific locales

1. I owe the insight about "common ground" to Andrew Rumsey's book *Parish: An Anglican Theology of Place* (London: SCM Press, 2017).
2. Robin Wall Kimmerer, *Braiding Sweetgrass: Indigenous Wisdom, Scientific Knowledge, and the Teachings of Plants* (Minneapolis, MN: Milkweed Editions, 2013), 23–24.
3. Kimmerer, *Braiding Sweetgrass*, 31.
4. These ideas are developed at length in Ched Myers, ed. *Watershed Discipleship: Reinhabiting Bioregional Faith and Practice* (Eugene, OR: Cascade Books, 2016).
5. This prayer appears in *Common Worship: Services and Prayers for the Church of England* (London: Church House Publishing, 2000), 291.

Thesis 10 In a time of widespread migration, Christians must embrace their identity as wanderers as well.

1. United Nations High Commissioner for Refugees, *Global Report 2022* (published June 2023) https://www.unhcr.org/what-we-do/reports-and-publications/global-report.
2. The Redeemed Christian Church of God, "Mission & Vision," https://www.rccg.org/mission-and-vision/.

Thesis 11 Public, shared places resist the dominance of the market. Building them up is part of Christian ministry.

1. Uber, "What Moves Us," https://www.uber.com/us/en/marketplace/.
2. Illinois Economic Policy Institute, "Improving Labor Standards for Uber and Lyft Drivers in Chicago," March 14, 2022, available online https://lep.illinois.edu/wp-content/uploads/2022/03/ILEPI-PMCR-Improving-Labor-Standards-for-Uber-and-Lyft-Drivers-FINAL.pdf and RideFair, "Legislated Poverty," February 2024 https://ridefair.ca/wp-content/uploads/2024/02/Legislated-Poverty.pdf.

3. The debate took place on September 26, 2016. The transcript is available online at https://www.nytimes.com/2016/09/27/us/politics/transcript-debate.html.
4. Robert Frost, "The Death of the Hired Man," first published 1914 in *North of Boston*, available online https://www.gutenberg.org/cache/epub/3026/pg3026-images.html.

Thesis 12 Food is at the center of the church and must be at the center of Christian witness.

1. Wendell Berry, "The Pleasures of Eating," originally published in 1989 and frequently re-published, including in Norman Wirzba, ed., *The Art of the Commonplace: Agrarian Essays of Wendell Berry* (Washington, D.C.: Counterpoint, 2002).
2. Again, I am indebted to Ellen Davis' reading of this passage in *Scripture, Culture, and Agriculture: An Agrarian Reading of the Bible* (Cambridge: Cambridge University Press, 2009), 66–79.

Thesis 13 In a mistrusting world, the church is called to be a community of responsibility and solidarity.

1. The interview took place on Sky News on June 3, 2016. It was widely reported at the time and video of the interview is available online at https://www.youtube.com/watch?v=GGgiGtJk7MA.
2. Musa Dube, "To Pray the Lord's Prayer in the Global Economic Era," *The Ecumenical Review* 49.4 (1997): 439–450.
3. Pope Francis, "Where is Your Brother?" Homily on the Island of Lampedusa, July 8, 2013 in *A Stranger and You Welcomed Me: A Call to Mercy and Solidarity with Migrants and Refugees*, ed. Robert Ellsberg (New York: Orbis Books, 2018), 4–7.
4. I owe the insight about the relationship of catholicity and solidarity to Kenneth Leech, *The Sky is Red: Discerning the Signs of the Times* (London: Darton Longman & Todd, 2003), 34.

Thesis 14 The church's future is an ecumenical one—but a very specific kind of ecumenism.

1. Anglican-Lutheran International Continuation Committee, *The Niagara Report: Report of the Anglican-Lutheran Consultation on Episcope, Niagara Falls, September 1987* (Anglican Consultative Council, 1988).

Available online at https://www.anglicancommunion.org/media/102175/the_niagara_report.pdf.
2. Third Assembly of the World Council of Churches (New Delhi, 1961), Report of the Section on Unity, para. 2. Available online at https://www.oikoumene.org/resources/documents/new-delhi-statement-on-unity.
3. I first heard this phrase associated with Ridley Hall, a Church of England theological college in Cambridge, but it may have originated elsewhere.

Thesis 15 The Eucharist sets the agenda for the church.

1. "Concerning the Service of the Church," *The Book of Common Prayer and Administration of the Sacraments and Other Rites and Ceremonies of the Church* (New York: Church Hymnal Corporation, 1979), 13.
2. We lack a recent, comprehensive, and accessible history of the ecumenical movement and its missiological reflection. Scott Sunquist offers a helpful overview of some of these themes in chapter five of his book *Understanding Christian Mission: Participation in Suffering and Glory* (Grand Rapids, MI: Baker Academic, 2013). The primary sources from this period repay careful reading.
3. This argument was articulated at length by Gregory Dix in *The Shape of the Liturgy* (New York: Harper & Row, 1945). His argument has been critiqued from several perspectives but its influence on Anglican liturgy remains immense.
4. Eucharistic Prayer C, *The Book of Common Prayer and Administration of the Sacraments and Other Rites and Ceremonies of the Church* (New York: Church Hymnal Corporation, 1979), 371.

Conclusion

1. Donald M. MacKinnon, *The Stripping of the Altars: The Gore Memorial Lecture and Other Pieces* (London: HarperCollins, 1969), 34.